DOG
HEROES

summersdale

DOG HEROES

Summersdale Publishers Ltd
46 West Street
Chichester
West Sussex
PO19 1RP
UK

www.summersdale.com

Printed and bound in Great Britain

ISBN: 978-1-84024-767-1

Substantial discounts on bulk quantities of Summersdale books are available to corporations, professional associations and other organisations. For details telephone Summersdale Publishers on (+44-1243-771107), fax (+44-1243-786300) or email (nicky@summersdale.com).

Disclaimer
All stories not directly contributed have been researched from sources in the public domain. Every effort has been made to ensure that all information and any quoted matter in these stories is correct. Should there be any omissions or errors in this respect we apologise and shall be pleased to make the appropriate amendments in any future edition.

DOG
HEROES

TRUE STORIES OF CANINE COURAGE

BEN HOLT

CONTENTS

ACKNOWLEDGEMENTS

Thank you to everyone who helped with gathering material and the research for this book. Special thanks go to Steve Jamieson and Janeta Hevizi, Tamsin Thomas at RNLI and Sue Nicholls at Penwith District Council for Bilbo's story; Jon Hastie, and Vicky Bell at The Guide Dogs for the Blind Association for Yaron's story; Karen Frith at Lake District Search-Dogs for Dottie's story; Neil Hamilton Bulger, and James Coles at Search and Rescue Dog Association Southern Scotland for Briar's story; Nicola Willis, and Jenny Moir at Hearing Dogs for Deaf People for Lye's story; Mike Townsend, and Vicky Bell at The Guide Dogs for the Blind Association for Tom's story; Gary Wickett, and Vicky Bell at The Guide Dogs for the Blind Association for Roz's story; Lizzie Owen, and Allie Hogsbjerg at Dogs for the Disabled for Bella and Frodo's story; Cheryl Smith, and Hannah at The Leaf Agency on behalf of Canine Partners for Orca's story; David Patterson at Search Dogs Essex for Archie's story; Dave Davies at Happy Dogs North East for Max's story; PC Neil Sampson, Katie Whitworth at Wiltshire Constabulary and Victoria Brown and Melinda Dziedzic at The Kennel Club for Anya's story; and Ted Wright for Bess's story.

INTRODUCTION

Anyone who lives with a dog will know what extraordinary creatures they are. Their capacity to provide love, loyalty and friendship to their owners is unparalleled in the animal kingdom. But some dogs go beyond the role of man's best friend when they act to save lives – and they can rightfully be called dog heroes.

This anthology includes some of the most astonishing, fascinating and heart-warming stories of dogs' heroic acts that have appeared in the media around the world, and also some moving first-hand accounts by people who have witnessed quick-thinking and resourceful canines in action.

The stories include working dogs, ranging from lifeguard dogs to guide dogs. Whilst these animals are remarkable for their intelligence, it's true to say that they are only doing as they are trained. However, in some cases, their loyalty and dedication leads them to act above and beyond their duties in order to protect humans. Even more amazing, perhaps, are the family pets and strays that have acted instinctively to save their owners and even strangers from danger.

WATER RESCUE

Many dogs enjoy having a splash around in the water, though not all of them are natural swimmers: bulldogs, for example, have heavy bodies and short legs, which makes it difficult for them to stay afloat. Boxers, greyhounds and Dobermann pinschers all struggle in the water due to their low body fat.

The medium-sized breeds that have water-resistant coats and webbing between their toes, however, are excellent swimmers and very at ease in the water, such as Labradors and golden retrievers, which are bred for the purpose of retrieving prey from the water. This would account in part for the large number of water rescues attributed to dogs of these breeds.

Newfoundlands are also great water dogs and have long been used as working dogs by fishermen and water rescue teams. When the *SS Ethie* was grounded off the dangerous coast of Newfoundland in 1919, one Newfoundland dog is reported to have saved 90 people from the icy water.

In many cases, water rescue stories involve dogs of breeds such as these, that have some inbuilt instinct to rescue people from drowning, or a natural affinity with water. But some are just loyal pets, of indiscriminate breed, who are determined to save their owners from danger.

 BILBO

Bilbo is a 14-stone chocolate brown Newfoundland who lives with his owner near Land's End in Cornwall, UK. What started out as a natural love for the water resulted in Bilbo becoming the world's first qualified surf lifeguard dog, who is credited with saving several lives…

Bilbo's owner, Steve Jamieson (known as Jmo), is the head lifeguard at Sennen Cove, a beach near their home. When Bilbo first came to live with him, Jmo understood the famous Newfoundland reputation for an affinity with water. Bilbo absolutely loved the water, and when he came to the beach with Jmo he enjoyed playing in the waves and swimming with the lifeguards.

After a while, Jmo realised that Bilbo could be a useful addition to the lifeguarding team at Sennen Cove and decided to train him to help out. Bilbo had to be put through the same swimming and fitness tests as the other lifeguards and learn how to swim in all types of sea conditions. He was soon swimming with skill and confidence and became a fully fledged member of the team – the world's first fully qualified surf lifeguard dog. But Jmo had also come up with a unique way of using Bilbo to help get the safety message across to beachgoers:

" We [the lifeguards] were then employed by the local council who had spent thousands of pounds producing sea safety signs advising the public about beach safety, the flag system and so on. Hardly anyone took any notice of these signs. I had an idea to have a coat made for Bilbo in red and yellow – the same colour as the flags we want bathers to swim between. It would also have the message 'swim between the flags' on it. When Bilbo went on patrol he would wear his coat, becoming an instant success with the public. "

As dogs are not allowed on the beach in the summer, Bilbo rides on the back of a quad bike across the beach, watching for bathers in trouble. The quad stops at intervals so that everyone can meet Bilbo and read the message on his lifejacket. The lifeguards also patrol on a motorised Rescue Ski; Bilbo rides on the sled at the back, from which he can leap off into the sea to assist struggling swimmers and tow them back to safety. Jmo organises regular demonstrations where Bilbo simulates rescues to illustrate the dangers of swimming in strong currents.

" We trained Bilbo to recognise when someone was in trouble in the sea, waving and shouting for help. Bilbo wears a harness under his coat onto which we would clip a buoyancy aid. He would, on locating the "casualty", swim out through the surf, towing the tube behind

him. He would then swim around the casualty, drawing the float close to them. When he felt their weight clutching the tube he would turn and tow them ashore. **99**

Perhaps Bilbo's distinguishing skill, though, is his ability to warn people of imminent danger in the water. One woman had changed into her swimming things in a remote cove and was heading into the water. Jmo advised her against going in, explaining that the currents had recently shifted and were extremely dangerous, but she ignored him and headed towards the water anyway.

66 *Without any prompting whatsoever, Bilbo sensed that she was going to get into the sea, and he simply took off spontaneously and ran back down the cliff path towards the woman on the beach, placing himself between her and the sea, actually standing on her feet. She shouted to me to call the dog off, but Bilbo would not move. However, the woman pushed past Bilbo, whereupon he raced into the surf to block her way. Only then did she realise how strong the current was, as she saw what a difficult time Bilbo was having in the powerful waves, so she did not go in.* **99**

Bilbo's intuition and perseverance had prevented the woman from getting into trouble and being swept away by the strong currents surrounding the cove that day. His bravery did not go unrecognised and the local and national press ran coverage of the story – Bilbo even appeared on national television.

Alongside his regular lifeguarding duties, Bilbo now tours schools in the area and further afield with Jmo, teaching children about beach safety and making sure they remember to 'swim between the flags'. He has become somewhat of a celebrity and receives lots of fan mail and presents from people all over the world. With over 250,000 people visiting Sennen's mile-long beach every year, Bilbo certainly has an important task on his hands in educating the beachgoers – and he seems to manage to put a smile on everyone's face while doing it!

To learn more about Bilbo's job and beach safety, go to **www.bilbosays.com**.

What makes Bilbo a good surf lifeguard dog?

Bilbo is a Newfoundland, a dog breed from Newfoundland in Canada that is perfectly adapted to cope with the water. They have a double coat: oily and waterproof on top, and fine-haired underneath for warmth and insulation. Their long, powerful legs give them extra swimming strength and their large, webbed paws act like paddles. With a large tail that acts as a rudder, ears that stick flat to the head when in the water to prevent liquid getting in, and a large lung capacity that gives them increased endurance, these dogs are excellent candidates for lifeguard training. The dogs have been credited with many rescues throughout the breed's history.

 ECHO

Echo lived with her owner Tish Smith on Mantoulin Island, Canada. She proved to be an invaluable canoeing companion to Tish on a five-day trip that almost ended in disaster…

As a keen but inexperienced adventurer, Tish planned a canoe trip on Lake Huron, the second largest of the North American Great Lakes and the third largest fresh water lake in the world. Echo, a shepherd-collie mix, had always seemed at home in the great outdoors and especially loved to swim, so Tish brought her along for company, thinking she would enjoy the trip. The trip lasted for five days and took in some astonishingly beautiful scenery, but at 6 a.m. on the final day their adventure took a turn for the worse.

Although it was summer, a huge storm suddenly engulfed the area, creating enormous waves that lashed their canoe. Tish tried to put a lifejacket on Echo, but Echo would not cooperate, instead nuzzling up to Tish. Tish spoke constantly to Echo while fighting for hours to keep the canoe upright, but it was eventually capsized by an enormous wave, catapulting them both into the freezing water. They thrashed helplessly in the raging waves as their equipment and canoe disappeared into the storm.

The pair remained in the water for the next 12 hours, during which time Echo never left his owner's side, providing reassurance to Tish and also helping to keep her warm. 'It was shocking how cold it was for July,' Tish later said. 'We swam around for hours. I thought we'd be OK, but it was so cold.' Although Tish was a qualified nurse, she was so worried about Echo not wearing a lifejacket that she failed to notice the onset of severe hypothermia in her own body. Suddenly she felt a warm and happy sensation rush over her, as she slipped into unconsciousness.

Luckily, Tish's canoe was discovered and the OPP Marine Search and Rescue Team and the Canadian Air Force Search and Rescue Team from Trenton were called out. Although an initial search found nothing, a crew on an aerial sweep over the area spotted Echo swimming in circles around Tish. They were pulled from the water by paramedics and taken to hospital, where Tish made a full recovery.

By the time the pair were found, they had drifted within striking distance of land. A dog's instinct in this situation would have been to swim to the safety of the shore but, in spite of this, Echo remained by Tish's side. Echo's dense coat stopped her own body temperature from dropping to dangerous levels, and the heat she had passed on to Tish slowed the progress of her hypothermia.

By refusing to leave Tish, Echo had saved her life twice over – by keeping her core temperature above the survival point and by attracting the attention of rescuers who may not otherwise have spotted Tish in the water. 'Without

Echo... there wouldn't have been a rescue,' said Tish, who learned a valuable lesson that day not to underestimate the potential dangers of the great outdoors.

🐾 FRISKY 🐾

Hurricane Katrina caused havoc and devastation in 2005 across the Gulf coast of the US, especially to the city of New Orleans. Eighty-year-old George Mitchell was at home with his dog Frisky just along the coast in Biloxi, Missouri, when the storm hit…

George had had Frisky, a schnauzer-poodle cross, for 19 years. He'd taken him in as a stray puppy and the two had become inseparable. Though Frisky was elderly and almost totally blind, he still had plenty of life left in him.

On the day Hurricane Katrina struck, George and Frisky were at home alone when the floodwaters quickly swamped their house in Biloxi, leaving them unable to escape. They clung to the only thing they could to keep them afloat – a mattress. After around four hours, George began to feel as though he couldn't hold on any longer, and started to lose his grip on the edge of their float. 'About four hours after I was treading water and all, I was about ready to let go, and I felt this peaceful feeling like this was it,' he later explained. Suddenly Frisky, who was on top of the mattress, rushed over to George and began to lick his face.

This display of affection gave George the determination to regain his grip on the mattress and keep holding on. 'It kind of snapped me out of it and I was able to come back.' Every time George began to lose strength and slip into the water, Frisky was there to nuzzle him and spur him on to stay alive. Eventually, the waters ebbed away just enough to allow George and Frisky to escape from their sodden home and, once outside, rescuers were able to pull them to safety.

George was adamant that, if it hadn't been for Frisky, he would have simply let go of the mattress and drowned in the murky floodwater in his home. In a later interview, he said that it was partly the thought of who would take care of his beloved dog if he died that kept him going. 'I couldn't ever express the closeness between he and I,' he said. 'Without him I wouldn't be here, I really wouldn't.'

🐾 YARON 🐾

Guide dog Yaron, living with his owner Jon Hastie in West Kirby, Merseyside, astonished everyone one summer by acting above and beyond his guide dog duties to rescue a little girl from danger…

Jon Hastie was on holiday with his brother, his brother's wife and their two young daughters in the Isles of Scilly. Yaron, Jon's black Labrador-golden retriever cross, came along to fulfil his usual duties of safely guiding his blind owner.

The family were spending the afternoon at the beach when Jon's niece Charlotte, aged seven, fell off her bodyboard into the sea. She quickly started to drift out of her depth and, despite the fact that she was wearing a life jacket, became increasingly distressed. She tried to grab hold of her bodyboard and get back on, but in her panic she splashed around, which pushed the board further away. Jon recounted what happened next:

> Yaron saw that Charlotte was distressed and jumped into the sea. He swam out to Charlotte and began to circle around her, so that she could grab hold of his collar, before swimming back to shore. Charlotte's dad helped to bring them both safely back to the shore and neither were hurt, just a bit soggy!

Yaron's brave and intelligent reaction had prevented the situation from becoming far more serious; he had understood the situation quickly and taken it upon himself to help the distressed girl. After the terrifying ordeal, Charlotte realised the important role Yaron had played in her rescue. Jon described how the little girl expressed her gratitude:

> 66 *Charlotte was over the moon with Yaron, telling anyone and everyone that he had saved her life. This isn't what a guide dog is trained to do but Yaron went beyond the call of duty and is certainly a winner to me and my family.* 99

Yaron was named Beyond the Call of Duty Guide Dog of the Year 2008 as part of the prestigious Guide Dog of the Year Awards. The award was presented by television presenter Peter Purves. Vicky Bell, a spokesperson for the charity The Guide Dogs for the Blind Association, commented, 'It is fantastic that Yaron's bravery has been recognised and we are able to celebrate his amazing achievement.'

JAKE

Four-year-old Labrador retriever Jake had never been considered the brightest dog in the pack, but he knew exactly what to do when he spotted that his young owner Tony was in danger…

Twelve-year-old Tony Bailey regularly swam with Jake in the Platte River in Nebraska, US. But one day, heavy rains had increased the river's flow and caused eddying currents to swirl across the channel. Tony jumped into the river in his usual swimming spot and was immediately sucked under the water and downstream. The unexpected force of the current and the rise in the level of the river meant that Tony was completely out of his depth and was being dragged further into the centre of the channel. He shouted for assistance, but there was no one nearby.

Just as he was pulled entirely under the water, he saw his pet Labrador, Jake, leap from the bank into the river. Tony was under the water for some time, but when he eventually resurfaced, Jake was swimming beside him. Tony caught hold of Jake's neck and allowed the dog to tow him back to the riverbank. Thanks to Jake's intervention and his extraordinary display of strength in pulling Tony along through the raging torrents of the river, Tony was able to scramble to safety.

After the brave rescue, Jake was praised by Tony's family and rewarded with a large bone. Diane, Tony's mother, commented that Jake wasn't renowned for his intelligence, and said she was astonished that he had had the presence of mind to jump in and save Tony. Even Tony said that Jake sometimes behaved strangely and often became confused when confronted with everyday objects. They both agreed, though, that Jake had demonstrated another side to his personality in the river that day; he proved that, while he might not have been the world's most intelligent dog, he could more than make up for it with his kind heart and his loyalty.

SWANSEA JACK

The black Labrador retriever dubbed 'Swansea Jack' made as many as 27 watery rescues during his short life in the 1930s...

Jack lived with his owner William Thomas at Padley Yard, Wales, on the western bank of the River Tawe, an area that was made derelict after Swansea's shipping industry shifted to the eastern side of the river.

In 1931, aged just one, the Labrador retriever made his first heroic rescue when a 12-year-old boy who was playing on the wharf fell into the water. As a puppy Jack had always been frightened of deep water (perhaps that would explain why he was so watchful of humans in the water) but as soon as he saw that the boy was in trouble he jumped in and dragged him back to the shallows, where the boy struggled ashore. Despite his timely action, Jack's bravery was not reported at the time.

Several weeks later, Jack performed a second successful rescue by saving a flagging swimmer from the nearby waters of North Dock. This time his actions attracted a small crowd, and his photo and an account of the rescue were printed in the local newspaper. He was awarded a silver collar by the city council for his efforts, and sprang to fame as a local hero.

By the age of five, Jack had made so many rescues that he was featured in the national newspapers. He won numerous medals for his service to humans, including two bronze stars from the National Canine Defence League, the 'Bravest Dog of the Year' award from both *The Star* newspaper and the *Daily Mirror* in 1936, and the 'Bravest Dog' category at Crufts. He was even presented with a silver cup by the Lord Mayor of London when he was taken on a nationwide tour. Later, Jack also helped to raise substantial amounts of money for charitable causes when his owner permitted the famous and wealthy to be photographed with him.

Sadly, on 2 October 1937, aged just seven, Jack died after accidentally eating rat poison. A memorial to this charismatic and courageous canine was erected near to his favourite swimming spot on the promenade in Swansea, near St Helen's Rugby Ground. It can still be visited today.

Labradors to the rescue!

It would seem that Labrador retrievers have a habit of diving in and coming to the rescue of people in danger of drowning.

On 1 May 2008, ten-year-old Labrador Penny leaped into the fast-flowing River Elwy in North Wales when she and her owner, Brenda Owen, spotted a woman who had fallen from her wheelchair into the water. Penny dragged the unconscious woman back to the bank, where Brenda was able to pull her to safety. A police spokesperson said, 'There's no doubt that her quick thinking and prompt action saved the woman's life.'

Nine-year-old Ryan Rambo was rafting on the Roaring Fork River in Colorado, US, when his raft hit a log and capsized. He was wearing a life jacket, but attempts by rescuers to reach him with ropes failed and he began to drift away downstream. Thirteen-year-old Chelsea Bennett was playing on the riverbank with her two-year-old yellow Labrador retriever, Zion, when she heard Ryan's screams. Her brave dog jumped into the river and towed Ryan back to the bank. Thanks to Zion's quick intervention, Ryan suffered only a small scratch in the ordeal.

DEFENDING PEOPLE FROM HUMAN ATTACK

Most dogs will act instinctively to protect their territory, either by barking to warn off an intruder or by attacking them. Certain dogs are bred specifically for guarding, such as German shepherds, pit bulls and Staffordshire terriers, and these are the most likely to attack in response to a perceived threat. That doesn't rule out other breeds though, particularly if the dog feels they are defending someone or something they consider to be part of their 'pack' – usually their owner or other people and animals they live with. This section tells the stories of some courageous dogs that came to the defence of humans in a violent situation, often at the risk of their own lives.

MAYA

When Angela Marcelino returned to her home in San José, California, in June 2007 she had no idea that her pit bull terrier, Maya, was about to save her life…

As Angela Marcelino opened the door to her house, she suddenly noticed a shape in the shadows. Before she had time to react, a man had appeared, pushed her violently into the house and followed her inside.

She screamed as loud as she could, but the man had already slammed the door shut behind him. He told her to 'shut up' and grasped her firmly by the throat, almost choking her. After she managed to scream a second time he tightened his grip. 'That's when I saw a white streak run in from the other room,' said Angela. 'His grip was so tight that I could only gurgle the words, "Maya, get him."'

Eventually, pit bull terrier Maya was able to distract the man sufficiently for Angela to hit the man in his groin, causing him to release his grip on her throat. Angela took hold of Maya's collar and the man left, realising that Maya would continue to protect Angela from the attack. Angela followed the man from a distance and watched as he climbed into a car, taking down his registration number before phoning the police.

When the police arrived Angela answered their questions and described how Maya had come to her rescue. She noticed that Maya had something red on her face, and at first the police were concerned that the dog had been injured. But the blood on Maya's face didn't belong to the dog – it had come from Angela's attacker. Although the police had some difficulty in restraining the feisty Maya, they were eventually able to take a sample of the blood for testing. Later, a suspect was arrested and his DNA matched the blood found on Maya's face. The brave dog had not only saved her owner's life, but had also helped to convict her attacker.

As far as Angela is concerned, Maya is a true hero. 'I'm so proud and grateful to have her as part of the family,' said Angela. 'It makes each day a little easier to deal with. We can't imagine life without her.' Maya was awarded The Animal Miracle Foundation's National Dog Day 'Hero Dog of 2008'.

Pit bulls – a dangerous breed?

The term 'pit bull' is used in reference to several breeds of dog, most commonly the American pit bull terrier, American Staffordshire terrier and Staffordshire bull terrier. Pit bulls have a reputation for being aggressive and dangerous, as these animals often fall into the hands of irresponsible people, who may only be interested in owning the dog because of the 'macho image' connected to them. Their bad reputation stems from their history as fighting dogs, and has been worsened by reports in the press of pit bulls that have attacked humans, including small children. In the UK, restrictions have been placed on the ownership of pit bulls under the Dangerous Dogs Act 1991, and some states in the US have laws restricting breeding and ownership. But as Maya's and two of the other dogs' stories in this section show, they can be loyal, loving and highly protective companions, especially if they are trained and handled properly.

✿ GRACIE ✿

In August 2008 in the US, the Ohio press reported that a 27-year-old woman living in the town of Springfield was woken by noises in her house…

Hearing noises in her house, a young woman in Ohio assumed it was her dog and went downstairs, to be met by a nasty surprise. She found a male intruder who had crept into the house and was attempting to steal her Xbox, DVDs and television. When she confronted him, asking what he was doing, things took a turn for the worse. The man grabbed hold of her, threw her down on the floor and started to attack her with a knife. He sliced a large gash on her leg and more on her stomach, arms and face. She tried to fight back by kicking him in the groin, but it had little effect and he continued the brutal assault, though he did cry out.

Perhaps that's what alerted the dog that something was wrong. Gracie, only two years old, ran downstairs and bit the attacker on the leg, causing him to run away, giving the woman an opportunity to telephone for help. Medics rushed her to hospital and she recovered, thanks to Gracie – who stopped a burglary from turning into something much worse.

 # UNNAMED GERMAN SHEPHERD

One Sunday evening, a woman came close to experiencing a nasty attack but was saved by her dog…

A woman in her forties was walking her German shepherd in the park in the Harrowgate Hill area of Darlington, County Durham. It was dark, but she let the dog off the lead and watched him closely. It was then she realised there was someone behind her. The woman turned and saw a man in a padded jacket, who then made a sudden movement with his arms and an obscene suggestion, leaving the woman shocked and terrified.

The German shepherd, extremely protective of its owner, started barking and growling and baring its teeth, then lunged at the man and sank its teeth around his right forearm. It refused to release his grip, even when the man violently tried to shake free.

The woman ran away as he was struggling with the dog, and then shouted for the animal once she was at a safe distance. It released the man, who ran off in the opposite direction.

Later, she was able to describe the man to police, who then monitored hospitals and health centres in the hope that the man would seek treatment for the bite.

AI KA

A factory worker from Bangkok described how her 14-year-old mixed-breed dog Ai Ka was injured when a man attacked her with a knife and a gun...

Tawee Makmee, a 42-year-old factory worker, was going home by motorbike when she spotted someone she knew, a man named To, arguing with a teenager. She stopped to ask what was going on, at which point the man became very angry, took out a knife and lunged towards Tawee with it.

'I ran to my house. But he broke in and pointed a gun at my head,' Tawee said. 'I was pleading for my life when my dog suddenly barked and jumped at the man.' The man then shot her dog, Ai Ka, twice.

'He pointed the gun back at me but I pleaded for my life and explained that I didn't intend to offend him from the very beginning,' Tawee said. 'After some time, he agreed to leave without hurting me.'

Immediately, she rushed her faithful defender Ai Ka to the vet, where the dog underwent an operation to remove two bullets from his leg, and was given calcium in the hope that his fractured bone would heal naturally.

'I am so sorry he was shot in place of me,' Tawee said. 'He saved my life.'

🐾 ANGEL 🐾

When a woman and her two-year-old son were threatened by a man with a knife, the last thing she expected was for a stray dog to come out of nowhere to her rescue…

A Florida woman had taken her two-year-old son to the playground in Port Charlotte and was just leaving when a man approached her with a knife and warned her not to make any noise or sudden movements. Not knowing what to do, she froze. Suddenly, she saw a pit bull terrier run up and bare his teeth, growling and barking at the man, who simply fled.

'You hear about family dogs protecting their owners, but this dog had nothing to do with this woman or her kid,' Animal Control Lt Brian Jones said. 'He was like her guardian angel.'

Badly trained pit bulls have brought the breed a menacing reputation, but this one seemed to have successfully thwarted a robbery and maybe even saved the life of this mother and toddler – even though the dog had never met them before. 'It was clear he was trying to defend this woman,' said Jones.

The woman got her boy into the car as fast as possible to drive away, but the dog jumped into the back seat. So, together with their guardian angel, they waited for the police and animal control officers to arrive.

There was still no sign of the owners, though the dog seemed healthy, so he was taken to a shelter and the woman he had rescued made it clear that she and her family would adopt him if he needed a home. After all, he was there when she and her son needed help. Not knowing his name, she simply called him Angel.

 KAISER

Craig Cunningham from Workington, Cumbria, who regularly looks after Staffordshire bull terrier Kaiser, was protected by the heroic dog when a man approached and demanded money…

Thirty-one-year-old Craig was out walking Kaiser behind the Moorclose Inn in Workington when a man wearing a hooded top appeared out of a back alley and asked for money. When Craig said that he didn't have any, the man drew a knife and started to attack. Kaiser leaped in to defend Craig, putting himself in danger, and the attacker then stabbed Kaiser with the knife.

'Anyone who knows Kaiser knows he's a good little jumper, and when he saw the lad come for me, he jumped in between us. I'll be honest – I ran off, I was really shaken,' said Craig of the frightening ordeal.

Unfortunately, the extent of the heroic dog's injuries were only discovered the following morning. By the time he was taken in to the vet's the next morning, Kaiser had lost a great deal of blood – six pints, in fact. He was rushed into surgery.

The next hours would determine whether Kaiser had lost his own life while protecting his guardian. Thankfully, he survived, and was returned safely to his owner, Ryan Charters from Moorclose. Craig applauded the dog's heroism, saying, 'He's been a little hero. If it wasn't for Kaiser I'd have been the one to get stabbed.'

BUFFY

Areas of East Oakland, the south-eastern and largest part of Oakland, California, US, have been plagued by high crime, violence and drug activity. Thankfully the Bartley family had Buffy to protect them…

One evening in January 2007, Will Bartley, owner of a mobile phone store near 92nd Avenue and International Boulevard, shut up shop and headed home. He had no idea that he was being followed.

The gunman who had trailed him home proceeded to rob him of $400, his credit cards and his ID. But Will's German shepherd dog Buffy, a family pet and 'true and loving friend' as Will described her later, wasn't going to let it happen. She leaped onto the gunman – who fired two shots, one hitting Buffy in her left front leg.

Buffy, seven years old, was bleeding as she was taken to a veterinary hospital. The vets managed to save her leg, but discovered she had a kidney problem that would be aggravated by the loss of blood. Complications took her back to the Bay Area Veterinary Specialists, but she stopped eating and grew weak. She only survived a month, and was put down.

That's not the end of the story, however. Buffy's heroic actions did not go unrecognised. The entire community showed their support with countless cards and letters of sympathy to Will and his family. The Humane Society of the United States chose to honour the German shepherd with the very first 'Dogs of Valor Award' in the companion dog category, to honour the extraordinary 'courage and dedication to her family' she had shown by intervening in the robbery.

It wouldn't bring her back, but Will and his family felt proud and grateful to their beloved Buffy. 'We still love and miss Buffy dearly.'

Dogs of Valor

The Humane Society of the United States created the Dogs of Valor Awards to give recognition to dogs that have performed an extraordinary act of courage by heroically helping a person in need. The second annual awards were held in May 2009 and the winner was Baby from Albuquerque, a five-year-old Great Dane that kept her owner warm for ten hours when he was trapped inside his SUV, which had plunged 20 feet down a hill and wedged between two trees, then went to get help. Firefighters were able to pull 82-year-old Elwood Cardon to safety and he was later treated for a cracked spine.

MANN

Surgeons should be recognised for their work in saving the lives of dogs which are injured in the course of defending their owners. This time, it was The Humane Society that helped one family through their ordeal…

Neil Chauncey was watching a movie at his home with six other family members one Thursday night in Mayport, Florida, when suddenly they saw three masked men approaching their house. Before they knew it, one of the men had burst through the front door, carrying a small shotgun.

Chauncey's pet pit bull, Mann, knew exactly what to do. He leaped up and managed to catch the burglar just as he was coming through the door. Unfortunately, it didn't stop the intruder, who kicked Mann off, turned the gun on the pit bull and in a cowardly act of malice shot him before running away with his partners in crime.

Chauncey and his family were saved. But what about Mann? Chauncey couldn't afford big vets' bills but he had to get help for the nine-month-old dog. He called all over town looking for assistance. Meanwhile, the pit bull was losing a lot of blood. Eventually, a clinic at Jacksonville Beach suggested he try the Clay County Humane Society. They promised to help the dog for free.

Doctors at the Humane Society took X-rays and discovered Mann's left front leg had been shattered by the bullet; they also found nerve damage. There was only one course of action: in an operation that took two hours, Mann's leg was amputated. The family, who stayed at the clinic throughout, learned that their pit bull would wake up from his sedation with only one front leg, but he would pull through after his traumatic experience and be back on his feet in days.

'He's going to have a long life,' said the surgeon, Doctor Alicia Price. Chauncey felt the dog had probably saved lives. 'If it weren't for him no telling what would have happened.'

GRACIE

Gracie was only a 50-pound puppy when a violent intruder entered her home and assaulted her owner, but in spite of her young age she acted with astounding speed and effectiveness in combating the attack…

Thirty-two-year-old mother of three Tonya Kendall was at her apartment in Imperial, Missouri, with her 11-month-old son playing with his toys on the living room floor, when she heard a knock on the door late one morning.

'Who is it?' she asked.

'Cable guy,' a man answered. Tonya remembered her neighbours talking about the problems they'd had with their cable the week before, so she opened the door.

She was unlucky.

The man pushed his way through the door and knocked her onto the stairs behind, pulled her T-shirt up and began to wrestle with her jeans. She later remembered that he smelled bad, a mixture of car engines and body odour, and was wearing a hooded sweatshirt and a cap. But his face was exposed as he held his gloved hand over her mouth.

Unable to move, suddenly at the top of the stairs above her she saw her young dog Gracie come to the rescue. The German shepherd lunged down the stairs at the man, landing on his shoulder and clamping its teeth into his flesh.

The attacker stood up and threw the puppy across the room. Tonya was devastated and frightened.

Gracie, however, was determined and undeterred. She charged again, this time locking on the man's right arm.

Again, he shook himself free and flung the dog back across the living room. But this time he wasn't waiting around for a third attack. As the dog came towards him again, he retreated out the door – with a threat.

'That's all right. I'll be back to finish what I started.'

Tonya Kendall locked the door behind him and at once grabbed her young child. She also found a baseball bat and a knife for self-protection. Then she sat down to telephone the police and her fiancé.

A knock at the door made her jump up with a start. Was her attacker back already? Would he force his way in, knowing that she could easily identify him, having seen his face? Mercifully, it wasn't him. It was the police.

The detectives with the Jefferson County Sheriff's Department showed her their badges and she described her attacker to a sketch artist – eyebrows, hair, eyes, and any distinguishing features. The drawing, when completed, made her physically sick, such was the trauma she had endured.

'It was him, in my house, all over again,' she said. 'But I can't completely fall apart. I've got three children. This man is not going to ruin my life. He's not. I won't let him.'

That night, trying to sleep, she imagined she could still smell the attacker in the room, although her fiancé reassured her she was safe. Her four-legged friend Gracie also climbed into the bed, ready to protect her whatever the cost.

🐾 DANTE 🐾

A dog's power to save lives, it seems, is not always in its teeth, as was proved by Dante, who helped to avert a disaster…

The Beaches district of Toronto, Canada, is usually known for its laid-back atmosphere and friendly neighbourhood where residents often walk their dogs near the shores of Lake Ontario. But one day James Paul Stanson, from the province of New Brunswick, loaded his car with several guns and 6,000 rounds of ammunition before driving there, with the plan of shooting as many people as he could.

On arriving in east-end Toronto, according to police, he went into a park to load his weapons. Then, astonishingly, he changed his mind when he met a playful dog, Dante, a part Husky, part Australian shepherd, which befriended him.

Stanson turned himself in to the police and was charged with eight weapons and firearms offences. Local resident Kristina Khyser, proud owner of the pet that may have prevented a terrible crime, was not surprised by Dante's behaviour.

'He's extremely empathetic,' she said. 'If one of my children cries he gets upset and so it doesn't surprise me he would sense first of all a dog lover, but a dog lover that's upset.'

 CALAMITY JANE

Though Calamity Jane had lost a leg due to a bullet wound, that didn't deter the gutsy dog from seeing off a group of armed robbers who were terrorising the neighbours...

Calamity Jane, a golden retriever, was discovered abandoned by the side of the road in Texas. Worse, her left front leg had a bullet wound and had to be amputated in order to save her life, and during the emergency surgery she was also found to be pregnant.

The dog was taken into care by Golden Retriever Rescue of North Texas. There, she adapted to life on three legs and gave birth to seven healthy puppies. Life was looking up for Calamity Jane. Or so you might have thought.

Her puppies were just a few weeks old when she somehow sensed trouble nearby. The Koleman family next door were being attacked by armed robbers and held at gunpoint that late January night. An unlikely hero, this three-legged golden retriever started barking at once, causing the robbers to flee – hotly pursued by Calamity Jane, who had good reason to be wary of guns, but wasn't going to be deterred even though she had lost a leg to one.

'Things could have turned out a lot different had it not been for her,' Steven Koleman told a local TV station. The Kolemans credited Calamity Jane with saving their lives.

 HSIAO HEI

A stray dog that was taken in and put to work as a security dog at a factory soon proved to be an asset to the company…

In Hsinchu County, Taiwan, factory security staff had adopted a dog called Hsiao Hei as their guard dog after finding him as a stray two years before and feeding him daily with their leftovers.

It was December 2007 when the dog became aware of someone nearby and began barking fiercely. The intruder misguidedly ignored the warning and continued to trespass onto the grounds of the closed factory.

Hsiao Hei bit the man on the thigh and crotch, then continued to attack the man and was gripping his right arm with his teeth to hold him prisoner when factory security arrived. The guard dog then watched him carefully in the security room while they waited for police to arrive.

Security staff were so proud of their heroic former stray. 'He doesn't bark that often, but we've finally realised his bravery in this experience which just proves the saying that "a dog's bite is worse than his bark".'

Hsiao Hei was rewarded with a chicken thigh for his courageous action. Meanwhile, the burglar, Shih Chin-lung, a wanted man for his previous burglaries, was met with giggles by the hospital nurse when police took him there for bite treatment.

SEARCH AND RESCUE DOGS

Specially trained dogs play a vital role within search and rescue teams around the world, whether they're finding people buried by avalanches and earthquakes or tracking down lost hikers.

People have been training and breeding dogs to use their superior senses of smell and direction to locate missing people for centuries. Perhaps the most famous type of rescue dog is the St Bernard, trained by monks in the Alps for winter rescue and credited with saving thousands of lives.

Air-scenting dogs are used by search teams to quickly cover large areas of ground, making their work much more efficient. Once they have found the target, these dogs are trained to return to their handler, give a special 'alert' signal, and then lead their handler back to the person.

Search and rescue dogs have to be tough to take part in difficult and often dangerous operations. Most well-suited are the larger breeds that are physically strong and agile, and have a keen sense of smell, such as German shepherds, golden retrievers and Belgian Malinois.

But our canine friends never cease to surprise us, and there are not a few tales of untrained and self-appointed 'rescue' dogs following their noses and their natural instincts to bring an endangered person to safety.

 BARRY

Barry lived from 1800 to 1814 and was trained as a mountain rescue dog by the monks at the monastery of St Bernard Pass near the Swiss–Italian border…

St Bernard Pass sits at just over 8,000 feet above sea level in the western Alps. The 49-mile path through the pass is only free from snow for a short period during the summer and it has always proved a treacherous route. Around 1050, an Augustine monk named St Bernard de Menthon founded a hospice and monastery in the pass and the monks later began to run rescue missions to save stranded trekkers after snowstorms.

At the start of the eighteenth century, servants were sent out to accompany travellers between the hospice and Bourg-Saint-Pierre on the Swiss side of the pass. By 1750, the servants were usually accompanied by dogs of what later came to be known as the St Bernard breed, which would walk in front of the travellers, clearing a path through the snow with their broad chests. These dogs had a highly attuned sense of direction and were well adapted to withstanding the extreme cold weather. Their acute sense of smell meant they were able to locate people buried deep in the snow.

The monks began to send them out in packs of two or three to search for lost or injured travellers. When they found someone injured buried in the snow, one dog would dig through the snow and lie on top of them to provide warmth, while another dog would return to the hospice to raise the alarm. Popular legend has it that the dogs carried casks of liquor strapped to their collars to revive freezing travellers, but there are no historical records of this practice. Over the course of nearly 200 years, the canines helped in the rescue of around 2,000 people, from lost children to Napoleon's soldiers.

One name stands out amongst these dogs: Barry, who is recorded as assisting in 40 rescues. His most famous and often cited rescue was that of a young boy who was stranded on an icy ledge. The story goes that Barry was sent down the precipice to the boy because none of the men in the rescue team could reach him. The boy was unconscious and covered in thick snow, which was still falling. Barry is said to have inched his way along the ledge towards the frozen boy, then started licking the child's face. After a time the boy was woken by Barry's warm licks and wrapped his arms around the dog's neck, allowing the strong dog to pull him up from the ledge and to safety.

When Barry died his body was preserved and is still on display today at the Natural History Museum in Berne, Switzerland, and a monument to him was erected at the entrance to the Cimetière des Chiens pet cemetery in Paris.

St Bernards – a breed with a history

The monks at Great St Bernard Hospice first acquired their famous dogs to serve as companions and watchdogs some time in the 1660s. They were descendants of the mastiff-style Asiatic dogs brought over by the Romans. This breed was smaller in size to the St Bernards we know today, and had shorter, reddish brown and white fur and a longer tail.

The breed living at the hospice was nearly wiped out between 1816 and 1818, when many dogs died in avalanches during particularly severe weather. In 1830 the monks began to experiment with cross-breeding the dogs with Newfoundlands, in the hope that the longer hair of this breed would help to protect them from the cold, but they soon discovered that ice would form on the longer hairs, making the dogs less effective in their rescues.

In 1855, innkeeper Heinrich Schumacher set up a breeding program. He supplied the hospice with dogs and also exported them to England, Russia and the US. The exported dogs were often bred indiscriminately with breeds such as English mastiffs. In 1880, the Swiss Kennel Club officially named the breed of dogs raised at the hospice as St Bernard.

In 2004, the Barry Foundation was formed and kennels were established in Martigny, a village near to the pass. On average, 20 St Bernard puppies are born there every year.

DOTTIE

Dottie and Karen of Penrith Mountain Rescue Team had attended all sorts of search and rescue missions, from train crashes to fallen climbers, but they had yet to make that crucial first find...

Karen Frith, a member of Penrith Mountain Rescue Team, covering the area of the north-east Lake District and northern Pennines, began to train her Border collie, Dottie, to work as a mountain rescue search dog in 2005. By February 2008, when Dottie celebrated her third birthday, she had been fully qualified for just over a year.

One cold evening the emergency pager went off, alerting Karen that her help was needed. Immediately Dottie, who was by now used to the routine of searches and the build-up to them, began to bark and jump up at Karen, as she made her preparations for the search.

I quickly grabbed a rucksack, made some sandwiches and a flask of tea and we left the house. All the pager said was "dogs required in search for missing male", so I drove straight to the rendezvous, the police station. On arrival I met up with four other dog handlers and all the dogs went through the usual rigmarole of greeting each other (which, for the male dogs, mainly involved peeing up the car tyres for several minutes!). We left them outside and went to be briefed by the local police. 🙦

They were told that they were looking for a gentleman who was on medication and required an oxygen supply. He had been missing from a nearby care home since earlier in the day. Dottie and Karen were allocated an area of woodland to search next to a large body of water. The night was rapidly closing in and there was no light other than their torches:

🙦 *We searched in lines through the densely overgrown woods, sometimes wading in water to our knees. It's eerie searching in woodland at night – you just catch a flash of light from the dog jacket and hear the bell jangling in the distance whilst the dog slips through the undergrowth. Your eyes try to become accustomed to the lack of light and you imagine all sorts of noises. The only consistent and comforting thing is your little collie, who will occasionally return to you and slip her nose into your hand as if to reassure you.* 🙦

That night the search was unsuccessful, and after about four intense hours the team stood down. The dogs were given the reward of a quick ball game before everyone went home for some rest before an early start the following morning.

After discussing the search with the police, it was decided that Dottie and Karen would concentrate on an area of woodland close to where they had searched the previous night. They began working through the woods, using a set compass bearing as their guide. After a few minutes, Dottie began to work further away; Karen couldn't see her but could hear the regular sound of her bell marking out her location.

> Suddenly I saw Dottie appear, running towards me with her tongue lolling and her tail wagging madly. She got within a couple of metres of me and barked loudly in excitement. Well, this is what we trained for, I thought – but was it real? Had she found the man we were searching for? I gave her the command to take me back to the casualty ("Show me!") and she ran back into the woods, zigzagging through the trees. When I caught up with her she was barking hysterically at some fallen wood. My heart sank – clearly she was just playing. Yet she wouldn't stop barking; she became so insistent that she ran to me and nipped at my trouser leg. I bent down and there, tucked right under a fallen tree, was our missing man. He was blue and extremely cold – barely alive, in fact. My little dog stopped barking and cuddled in close to the casualty as if to try and help me warm him.

After the initial shock of finding the man and dealing with the immediate first aid, Karen called for assistance from the other searchers. Soon they had him stabilised and on a stretcher, and carried him to a waiting ambulance. Dottie would not leave the man until he was handed over to the paramedics and was certain that he was safe. The man had a great deal to be grateful to Dottie for – had it not been for the tenacity of the little black and white collie, the man could easily have died of exposure. Karen had nothing but praise for little Dottie:

66 *My pride in my dog is immense; the loyalty, commitment and perseverance she shows when on searches – in all weathers, any condition and even late at night – is amazing. She does it for me but she also does it because she loves it. I will always be in awe of her.* 99

Sniffing out a missing person

Scent plays an important role in locating a missing person, and dogs can be trained to sniff out any human body or corpse in a large area, or even a particular person if they are first given a scented article such as a piece of clothing.

Research is ongoing, but dogs are thought to be able to pick up on the tiny traces left behind by humans, such as evaporated perspiration, skin rafts (scent-carrying skin cells – roughly 40,000 of these drop off a human's skin every minute), respiratory gases or decomposition gases.

When a search team have identified a probable location for a subject, air-scenting dogs can be deployed to that area and used to quickly pinpoint them. To qualify for the job, they have to prove they are able to work for four to eight hours at a time without distraction – i.e. without chasing any wildlife in the area! Their handlers have to know their stuff, too; they need to be skilled in navigation and wilderness survival techniques, and be self-reliant as it can be lonely work.

STUB

Ludivine was out walking her dog Stub when the pair stumbled into the middle of a search and rescue operation...

Ludivine Cauchon often took her seven-year-old Labrador retriever, Stub, for walks in a wooded area near their home in Château-Richer, Quebec. Earlier on the day in question, Marise Boucher and Christian Lachance had been out walking close by. There had recently been a snowstorm, and as they passed through a ravine the weight of the unstable fresh snow caused an avalanche. The snow that had built up along the sides of the ravine collapsed, burying the two teenagers.

When Ludivine came across the rescue team that was looking for the teenagers, she wanted to help. So she volunteered Stub, her trained hunting dog, to assist in the search. Remarkably, only moments later Stub uncovered a pair of gloves.

The rescue team took this clue and set to work. Sure enough, Christian and Marise were found huddled together under the snow and were rushed straight to hospital. Marise was treated for multiple injuries and severe hypothermia and made a full recovery, but tragically Christian did not survive. Though the event was tempered with sadness at the loss of Christian, Marise and her family all expressed deep gratitude to the dog that had helped save her life.

🐾 BRIAR 🐾

Search dog Briar was off duty and enjoying a walk with her handler, Neil Hamilton Bulger, when the pair made an unexpected discovery…

It was May 2007 and Neil Hamilton had been walking Briar, a trained search dog, on the fells close to High Corrie on the Isle of Arran. On returning from the summit of the fell, Neil decided to take a shortcut and headed north along a forestry fence. After ten minutes or so, Briar ran off in the opposite direction to Neil, a few hundred metres along the path from where they had just come. Some minutes went by and Briar came bounding back towards Neil.

> *I thought this was very strange, as she always likes to keep me in sight, apart from when she is working. She started indicating to me, as she would when she is working and has found a person. When we are out walking she picks up people's scent quite often, but she just stands rigid with her nose in the air for a few seconds and then continues on. When we work the dogs we put them in jackets or specially designed harnesses; it puts them into a frame of mind that would best be described as "working mode".*

The difference between 'working mode' and just a normal walk is an important distinction for working dogs; for example, when a helicopter flies over Neil's house, Briar is often known to run and hide under the bed. When she has her working jacket on, however, she is eager to be the first to climb into the helicopter to be taken to the search site. On this day, Briar was behaving as though she was on a search and rescue mission, even though she wasn't wearing her jacket.

> *To start with I thought Briar was mucking about and told her to stop being silly and tried to get her to walk on. But she wouldn't have it; she was barking and jumping up, and when I tried to move away she wouldn't let me. So, I thought I would just play along and I told her to show me what she had found.*

As soon as Neil had given this instruction, Briar raced back off in the direction she had come from. Neil followed her down into a gully, to a stream called the Corrie Burn.

> *When I arrived there was Briar, standing next to a man, who was sitting in a heap next to the burn. He was in quite a bad way – his face was covered in blood and he was very dazed. From what I could get from him he had gone for a drink from the burn and fallen in face first. He had taken the impact to his hands and face.*

After Neil cleaned him up with dressings from his first aid kit the man wanted to make his way back to the path. They walked down the fell and found a seat near to a track. While Neil was phoning for an ambulance, the man's wife appeared on the track with her car and took him to hospital herself. The 57-year-old walker later discharged himself from hospital after treatment for a broken nose and facial lacerations.

> *I don't know why Briar decided to take it on herself to find the man and let me know. Maybe she smelt the blood or a certain scent that she recognised as fear, I just don't know. A few weeks later a "thank you" letter arrived at our business, addressed to Briar, with a bank note to buy her a squeaky toy (her usual reward for finding someone).*

Briar has since found two other people whilst on duty for the Arran Mountain Rescue Team.

KENO

Keno, a five-year-old Labrador retriever from British Columbia, was another dog that helped make a dramatic rescue after an avalanche...

Ryan Radchenko, a ski lift operator at Fernie Alpine Resort in Fernie, British Columbia, was skiing off-piste on the day before the resort opened to the public for the season when tonnes of snow broke loose from a ridge and tumbled down on top of him in the Currie Bowl. The area where Ryan was buried was fairly small, but that still didn't leave the rescue team much time.

Robin Siggers, head of the Fernie Alpine Resort mountain rescue team and in charge of four canine rescue dogs, including Keno, at the time of the accident, explained, 'Statistically they say you have about a 50 per cent chance after 30 minutes. Less than four per cent of people ever survive being buried more than two metres deep. Once you're six feet down, you're as good as gone because it's going to take half an hour to dig you up.' Within two minutes of being dispatched onto the scene, Keno had found Ryan's glove, allowing the team to locate Ryan and dig him out. He was unconscious and buried under one metre of snow with his hand reaching above him – he had been trapped for just 26 minutes.

Ryan was rushed to hospital, but was back safe, sound and well on site after an hour, to the huge relief of Siggers and the rest of the staff. A wooden plaque from the Canadian Avalanche Rescue Dogs Association was hung above Siggers' desk. It read: 'First Live Find. Congratulations Keno and Robin.'

Intensive training for precise results

Avalanche rescue dogs are put through intensive training before being taken out on the slopes on assignment. Part of the training involves fetch and tug-of-war games, which may look like fun to watch, but are a vital part of the learning process.

The dogs then practice with scented articles. The scenarios get more difficult and complicated as the dog progresses through the training, until they are able to find articles that have been buried 70 centimetres down and left out overnight. The dogs also have to learn how to ride on chairlifts, snowmobiles and helicopters to convey them quickly to avalanche sites.

When a dog performs its 'digging' alert it means it has found a person. Their scent may have meandered slightly on the way up through the layers of snow, so the dog might not be directly above – but close enough for handlers to come in and use their probes to pinpoint the person. A line of searchers acting without a dog could take hours to find someone using just their probes – hours that the trapped individual cannot afford.

BOZ

Faithful Labrador Boz stayed by 74-year-old Mark Corrie's side for two days when he was lost in bad weather on the Cumbrian hills....

One Saturday morning, Mark Corrie, from Greenhill, Cumbria, set off to walk his daughter's Labrador, Boz. When unexpected bad weather set in he became disorientated and strayed off the path. He sheltered in a dip in the ground while Boz stood on a ridge on Cumrew Fell, barking in alarm.

When Mark was reported missing by his family, a major search operation ensued, involving 45 volunteers from mountain rescue teams across the north of England. By the next day, 97 people had been enrolled in the search effort, including police underwater search teams, dog search teams and a helicopter from RAF Boulmer equipped with heat-seeking thermal imaging cameras. But it was Boz's incessant howling, rather than any of this highly technical equipment, that finally alerted searchers to Corrie's location on the Monday, two days after he had gone missing.

'I am so relieved. Boz is great,' said Mr Corrie's wife, Pat. 'A friend from the village heard the dog barking on the ridge. She decided it was in distress so she and her husband went to look. The dog ran to them, then ran away and took them to Mark.'

Mr Corrie was suffering from dehydration when he was found, and was airlifted to hospital by the Great North Air Ambulance Service. It just so happened to be his 74th birthday on the day he was saved – Boz had certainly given him a birthday present to remember by helping the rescue team to find him in time! 'Boz is a hero,' said Mrs Corrie. 'He is enjoying all the attention – and getting lots of treats.'

HORTON

Horton, a seven-year-old Labrador and the Pfau family pet, knew Quandry Peak so well that rescue teams would often call on him for assistance when someone was lost and in danger on the mountain…

David Pfau was a professional photographer who lived near to the base of Quandry Peak, a 14,000-foot mountain in Colorado. His dog Horton had been hiking to the summit on photography trips with him ever since he was a few months old. Horton loved the outdoors so much that he would often go out on his own hikes, joining other hikers and accompanying them to the top – well, those that could keep up with him! 'Horton knows this trail better than anybody,' said David Pfau. 'He's in love with this mountain.'

He became a well-known figure amongst hikers, and local search and rescue teams would sometimes stop at the Pfau family home to enlist his help. Though Horton was not a trained search and rescue dog, he contributed to saving the lives of at least three people on Quandry Peak. The weather can change very quickly at such high altitudes, going from a sunny day to snowy conditions within minutes, and one man found himself lost in a snowstorm. Luckily, Horton was there and was able to guide him safely down the mountain. The man later came to the Pfau family home to thank them. 'The one man who came to our door to tell us that Horton saved his life said he couldn't see where he was going,' said Emily Pfau, David's wife. 'He told us he could see his feet, and Horton's tail, and so he just followed Horton the whole way down.'

🐾 SUZIE 🐾

A firefighter's dog from Texas named Suzie helped a man who found himself in a sticky situation out on Eagle Mountain Lake…

Firefighters from the Newark Volunteer Fire Department were called out to Eagle Mountain Lake in Texas when an unnamed man became trapped in the mud 500 feet from the bank. Amongst them was Chris Cromer and his Labrador retriever, Suzie.

Cromer supervised as Suzie took the man supplies of hot packs and blankets to help keep him warm and fight off hypothermia until he could be pulled to the bank by rope.

Cromer said that Suzie's actions on that day were just typical of her generous and helpful nature: 'If I eat a plate of food in the living room, she takes the plate to my wife in the kitchen. She'll go get my remote for me for the TV.'

Suzie also helped to calm the man's infant son as the man was being pulled to safety by the rescue team.

🐾 CHARCO 🐾

Charco, a black Labrador retriever and sniffer dog that saved a man's life after the Kashmir earthquake in 2005, was given a hero's welcome when he returned home to the UK...

The Kashmir earthquake of 2005 struck on 8 October, with its epicentre in Pakistan near the border with India. An eight-man sniffer-dog rescue team from Llanfairfechan, Wales, known as BIRD (British International Search and Rescue Dogs) was dispatched to work in Muzaffarabad, one of the worst hit areas. This was as part of a wider 38-strong British rescue team sent to Pakistan.

The team from north Wales pulled a 20-year-old man from the wreckage of a collapsed building after Charco indicated that he had found someone buried beneath the rubble. The man had been trapped for 54 hours and at that stage in the rescue process was one of only two people recovered alive in the area.

His handler, Neil Powell, described how Charco, nine years old at the time, had to work in some highly treacherous conditions, but never once refused to complete his duties.

'We arrived at a row of buildings which looked like they could collapse at any minute,' said Mr Powell. 'The heat was intense and Charco squeezed into a passage full of rubble. Despite continuing aftershocks, he went to a corner and started barking.'

After his heroic stint abroad, Charco had to spend six months in quarantine before being returned to Mr Powell's home at the foot of the Mournes, near Newcastle, Co. Down, Northern Ireland. This wasn't the first time either – he'd already had to go through quarantine after assisting at an earthquake in Algeria in 2003, in which more than 2,000 people died.

'Since he has been home, he hasn't let the others out of his sight and his tail has never stopped wagging,' Mr Powell said.

The dog's international career was at an end – he would be working on home territory from now on. 'At home in Northern Ireland he helps the Fire Service in search and rescue and once cut his feet badly on glass at a gas explosion,' said Mr Powell. 'Despite the bandages, he still wanted to get back to work.'

Charco was shortlisted for *The Sun* Hero Dog Award, part of the Dogs Trust Honours 2009.

PROTECTING PEOPLE FROM DANGEROUS ANIMALS

For some dogs, the instinct to protect their pack and territory knows no limits. There is something deeply touching about a dog putting its own life at risk and taking on an animal much larger than itself, such as a bear or wolf, or a potentially deadly creature such as a snake, in an attempt to protect its human owner from harm. Even more striking, though, is when a dog acts in this way in defence of a person it barely knows. The acts of bravery described in the stories in this section go far beyond what any family would expect of their loyal pet.

 TESS

Fay Palethorpe and her kelpie, Tess, had a close call one Sunday morning when they came across a deadly eastern brown snake in their garden...

Retiree Fay Palethrope, aged 68 at the time, was in the garden of her Tallebudgera Valley home on Australia's Gold Coast with her one-year-old kelpie pup, Tess, and her two other kelpies, when she spotted a snake lying on a rock. At about 1.8 metres in length, it was the biggest she had ever seen. It reared up the instant it saw Fay and lunged at her. As Fay screamed out and turned to run, the three dogs darted in front of her and began attacking the snake.

Fay's immediate response was to call the dogs off – from its brown scales she guessed the snake might be a poisonous eastern brown, and knew that a bite to one of her pets could be fatal. Two of them obeyed her command, but the youngest, Tess, continued her attack on the reptile, throwing it back and forth through the air. Then there was a sudden yelp – Tess had been bitten on the ear.

The injured snake managed to slither away in the confusion that followed, but now Fay's attention was focussed on getting her brave dog to the vet in time to save her. As it was a Sunday morning she had to ring around for an emergency vet, and Tess was in a bad way by the time they reached the surgery in Tugun. She was administered antivenin and put on an intravenous drip to try and flush the rest of the poison out.

Fay had to borrow money from her son in order to pay the emergency treatment bill, even though there was no guarantee that Tess would recover – but it was worth it for the dog that had saved her life. Fay lives alone on her 20-acre property – had she been bitten, it could have been too late by the time she was able to receive treatment. The eastern brown snake has fast-acting venom and is the second most venomous land snake in the world; though most patients respond well to the antivenin, about 50 per cent do not recover.

🐾 UNNAMED DOG 🐾

Puzhandi was away from home when he received a surprise phone call from his neighbour, who told him to turn on the news and watch a clip of his Dobermann defending the family property from a deadly cobra…

When Puzhandi's Dobermann spotted a 7-foot cobra trying to sneak into his owner's home in Chennai, India, a fierce battle on the lawn ensued, attracting a small crowd of onlookers from the neighbourhood. The crowd watched, enthralled, as the cobra, hood raised and hissing, dodged in between plants. The dog skilfully darted about just out of reach, before finally moving in for the attack and grasping the snake between its teeth, smashing it against the ground until it died. The fearless dog subsequently became somewhat of a local celebrity – the battle had been filmed and broadcast on news channels.

It was unfortunate that the cobra had to die rather than being humanely removed: cobras feed almost entirely on other snakes and only attack humans if provoked or in a situation where they are trapped and feel threatened. Had the snake entered the property it could have posed a danger to the unsuspecting family when they returned home. Dobermanns are for the most part a gentle, loyal and highly intelligent breed, but they will attack in response to a perceived threat to themselves, their territory or family.

🐾 GEORGE 🐾

Size does not matter where bravery is concerned; a fact demonstrated by the Jack Russell from New Zealand that defended a group of children from attack by a pair of aggressive pit bull terriers…

Nine-year-old Jack Russell George was playing with five local children, aged between three and 12 years, as they made their way home from buying sweets when they came across two aggressive pit bull terriers. Little George quickly jumped into action, barking ferociously to warn the dogs to back off, then shielding the children by taking the brunt of the attack as the dogs moved in.

He sustained horrific injuries, and it was the sad decision of his owner, Alan Gay, to have the suffering animal put to sleep. The two pit bulls were later surrendered by their owner to dog control officers and destroyed. The incident stirred up huge international interest and Mr Gay received telephone calls from hundreds of people who were touched by the story and wanted to offer their condolences.

George was later honoured with a posthumous PDSA Gold Medal, the animal equivalent of the George Cross, at a moving ceremony in his home town of Manaia, South Taranaki, New Zealand. The medal was handed to Alan Gay by Governor-General Anand Satyanand, then hung around the neck of a statue of George erected in the town in his memory. Director General of the PDSA, Jan McLoughlin, paid tribute to George, saying: 'There's no doubt that George was a small dog with a lion's share of courage. Each account of his devotion to the five children on the day of the incident tells of a dog that was not afraid to face great fear in order to protect his friends.'

A big dog in a small package

Jack Russells, or Jack Russell terriers, were first bred in England in the nineteenth century as working dogs, and used to flush foxes out of their dens during fox hunts. They are sturdy, tough little dogs with lots of energy, and can be hyperactive – though small they require as much exercise as dogs of larger breeds. Jack Russells can become stubborn and aggressive towards other animals and humans if they are not adequately socialised, so obedience training is essential. The feisty little canines are known for their tendency to take on opponents much larger in size than themselves. If cared for and properly trained, their energetic nature makes them excellent and long-term companions, with many living until their late teens.

🐾 SHADOW 🐾

Most of us were afraid of the 'big bad wolf' in fairy tales when we were little, but few parents nowadays are confronted with the horror of a pair of hungry wolves closing in on their children…

It was 22 December and the Keays family and their friend Rod Barrie were on a pre-Christmas tobogganing outing about 100 kilometres from Fort Nelson, Canada.

It was 3.30 p.m. and darkness was beginning to fall when Shadow, the Keays' Rottweiler cross and family pet, suddenly wrenched his lead out of the hands of Mrs Keays and bounded across the snow in the direction of one of the sleighs, aboard which sat her three young children. She let out a scream of terror when she saw the reason for Shadow's determined running: two wolves had appeared from nowhere and were fast closing in on the sleigh.

Father Kyle Keays, who was riding an ATV, or quad bike, some distance away, saw Shadow intercept the lead wolf. It hit Shadow in the shoulder, who quickly spun round and grabbed it by the face. Keays was too far away to help and so hurried off towards his work camp nearby to get a rifle. Rod Barrie, who was towing the children in the sleigh when the wolves approached, managed to remain calm and continue towards his truck, which was parked not far away, his wife sitting inside.

When he reached the truck the wolves were just 6 metres away: he and his wife pulled their terrified children into the safety of the truck. Armed with a shovel, Barrie began swiping at the wolves to keep them at bay. By now Barrie had had a good look at the wolves and could see their bones were protruding: they must have been starving. Shadow continued to growl at them, but they stood their ground, until Barrie jumped on his ATV and succeeded in driving them away some 20 metres, allowing them to get Shadow inside the truck and drive away.

Back at Keays' work camp they examined Shadow – he'd been lucky enough to escape with minor cuts and bruises. But the hungry wolves hadn't given up; a short while later the lead wolf appeared at the camp. Keays, a licensed hunter, was able to track the wolf and shoot her. He later found and shot the second wolf.

It is highly unusual for wolves to prey on humans, and in all his years of hunting Keays said he'd never had such a close encounter with these elusive animals. Luckily, Shadow was with them when the surprise attack happened, and his protective instincts prompted him to save the day.

The Legend of Gelert

In the village of Beddgelert, North Wales, a touching tribute to a brave and faithful hound is engraved on the supposed grave of Gelert, the famed favourite hunting dog of Prince Llewellyn. It reads:

'In the thirteenth century, Llewellyn, Prince of North Wales, had a palace at Beddgelert. One day he went hunting without Gelert "The Faithful Hound" who was unaccountably absent. On Llewellyn's return, the truant stained and smeared with blood, joyfully sprang to meet his master. The prince alarmed hastened to find his son, and saw the infant's cot empty, the bedclothes and floor covered with blood. The frantic father plunged the sword into the hound's side thinking it had killed his heir. The dog's dying yell was answered by a child's cry. Llewellyn searched and discovered his boy unharmed but nearby lay the body of a mighty wolf which Gelert had slain, the prince filled with remorse is said never to have smiled again. He buried Gelert here. The spot is called Beddgelert.'

BERRY

When pregnant Julie Closuit took her dog Berry out for the usual morning toilet break, she wasn't expecting a dramatic confrontation with a grumpy moose…

Every morning, before Julie would take her three-year-old Rottweiler Berry out to go to the toilet, she would first check for the neighbour's dog or any stray moose in the vicinity of her home in Fairbanks, Alaska. This morning was no different, and after looking around the corner of the house with her flashlight in the dark Julie, six months pregnant at the time, decided it was safe to bring the dog out.

A short while later, Berry began barking frantically. Julie assumed it must be the neighbour's dog, but as she shone her flashlight in the direction the dog was barking she revealed the silhouette of a moose behind a spruce tree about 20 feet away. She saw its ears go back and it began to charge towards them. Before she had chance to decide what to do, Berry yanked the leash out of her hand and rushed off towards the moose, circling behind it in a C-shaped herding pattern.

Julie followed the advice her parents had always given her in the event of such a situation – she dived behind some birch trees for protection in time to see the moose run past where she had been standing.

Berry rejoined Julie as she pulled herself up, just as the moose began its second charge. But Berry put herself between her owner and the moose, barking ferociously until the moose began to retreat back towards the house. As it did so, Berry ran over and headed it off, forcing it to turn back in the direction of the woods. Berry continued to bark until she seemed sure that the moose wasn't coming back.

Rottweilers are most commonly used as guard dogs, but originally they were bred for herding animals – perhaps this explains Berry's response and fast action. Though the whole incident probably only lasted 30 seconds, it made a lasting impression on Julie Closuit, who subsequently erected a fence on her property in the hope of preventing future altercations with the local moose population.

During the winter, when they're hungry and their energy levels are low, moose can become aggressive and are less likely to retreat if they see a human.

ASSISTANCE DOGS

For people who are hearing or sight impaired, an assistance dog can vastly improve their quality of life; not just by guiding them and helping them to complete everyday tasks, but by providing important emotional comfort and companionship. For many, an assistance dog gives them the confidence to carry on with a normal life despite their physical difficulties. The bond that develops between a person and their assistance dog is incredibly strong and, as the stories in this section show, that can sometimes lead to the dog doing something above and beyond their duties in order to ensure the safety of their owner.

LYE

Life took a turn for the worse for Nicola Willis when she became severely deaf, but her canine companion gave her the confidence to enjoy life again and was at her side in times of need…

66 *When I became deaf I withdrew into myself; became depressed and lost all confidence. What really upset me was that I became reliant on other people: I had lost my independence. I stayed in my house, but even that was awful as I just couldn't hear even simple sounds. I was sinking fast.* 99

She decided to apply for a hearing dog and was delighted when her own 14-month Cavalier King Charles spaniel, Lye, was assessed by the charity Hearing Dogs for Deaf People and accepted for training. The pair were separated for a difficult four months while Lye was put through her paces at training school, where she learned how to react to various household sounds including the telephone, doorbell, cooker timer and the 'call' (an instruction other people can give to Lye asking her to fetch Nicola), as well as the danger sounds of the smoke alarm and fire bell. In July 2005 they were reunited, this time with Lye in her smart, burgundy hearing dog working jacket. Since having Lye as a hearing dog, Nicola's life has changed dramatically.

" *When Lye came back to me having been trained, everything changed. Friends started to call on me again, knowing that not only would the front door be opened, but on the other side of the door would be two very happy individuals. It was like the light was shining again. My depression was lifting.* "

But Lye's dedication to Nicola didn't stop there. In 2008 Lye acted above and beyond the call of duty twice. The first time was on an outing to the shops; Nicola was recovering from a damaged knee at the time and was using crutches.

" *We were taking a shortcut through an alleyway when I fell over, and I just lay on the ground, cold, scared and in pain – I couldn't get up. To my surprise Lye ran off, which upset me even more as she was wearing her hearing dog coat and I thought she might get stolen. After a few minutes I looked up and saw my beloved dog running back to me with a man following close behind her. He told me she had gone to the main street and grabbed him by the trouser leg. He saw her coat and realised she must be telling him something so he followed her. It turned out that he was a nurse, so Lye picked well!* "

Lye's second act of bravery came one night when Nicola and her daughters were asleep in bed. Nicola had taken her hearing aids out to go to sleep and was woken by Lye scrabbling at her chest. At first she thought Lye might need the toilet so she started to get out of bed, but Lye pulled her back down and would not let her move. This was very strange behaviour for Lye, and it was enough to alert Nicola to the fact that something was wrong. Although her hearing aids do not fully restore her hearing, as soon as Nicola put them in she could hear noises she knew must have been coming from downstairs and realised there were intruders in her house.

> I panicked and didn't know what to do, but Lye just looked at me and told me in her own way that she would not let any harm come to me or my girls. Then she made enough noise to scare the burglars away, even after one of them gave her a vicious kick as he fled.

Lye's heroic actions have won her national recognition. She was runner-up in the Heroic Hearing Dog of the Year Awards in 2008, and she was chosen to appear in a calendar being issued by a national dog magazine. Lye has progressed from being a much-loved pet dog to being an invaluable lifeline, as Nicola sums up:

> Lye is my constant and faithful companion, and a very special dog. She is my ears and she has given me back my confidence and courage.

Hearing dogs

In 1975, Agnes McGrath and the Minnesota Society for the Prevention of Cruelty to Animals developed a hearing dog programme, which led to the establishment of the first institution to train dogs for hearing-impaired people: International Hearing Dog, Inc. Hearing Dogs for Deaf People was founded in the UK in 1982, with the aim to 'offer greater independence, confidence and security to deaf people by providing dogs trained to alert them to chosen everyday sounds.'

Hearing assistance dogs go through three to twelve months' training before they are assigned to a hearing-impaired person. They can be of any breed, provided they pass an initial assessment, which checks whether they have the right temperament, are reactive to sounds and willing to work. If they fulfil these criteria, they receive obedience training and are taught how to act in various public scenarios, such as in a lift, on public transport and how to interact with different types of people.

After their 'social' training they move on to sound alerting. They are taught to give their handler a physical alert on hearing certain sounds, such as doorbells, smoke alarms, ringing telephones, sirens and a person calling the handler's name. They may also be trained to lead their handler away from a warning sound such as a fire alarm. The dogs are easily recognisable by their distinctive burgundy jackets, which helps to identify their handler's otherwise 'invisible' disability.

 TOM

The bond between a guide dog and his 59-year-old owner was tested to the extreme during the terrorist attacks that took place on 7 July 2005 in London…

At around 9.45 a.m. on 7 July 2005, Mike Townsend from Leicester and his guide dog, Labrador-retriever cross Tom, were near Tavistock Place on their way to a business meeting, when there was a massive explosion close to where they were walking. A double-decker bus had been targeted by a suicide bomber and the resulting explosion totally destroyed the top rear section of the vehicle, killing 13 people and injuring many others. There was mayhem all around, but Mike had no idea as to what had happened due to his sight loss. At first he thought it may have been demolition work, but when he started hearing the sirens of emergency vehicles passing close by him, he quickly realised that he and Tom were in the middle of a serious incident. In their desperation to get away from the area where the bomb had gone off, people started rushing past and bumping into the bewildered Mike and poor Tom.

Almost as quickly as the panic had begun, it receded again. The area they were in became quiet and the streets deserted; the police had closed off many of the surrounding roads and the crowds had moved further from the scene of the explosion, leaving Tom and Mike alone and frightened.

However, despite the intense noise and panic, then the eerie desertion of the streets, Tom remained unfazed, and began to lead Mike away from Tavistock Square. Every time Mike and Tom came up to a roadblock Tom would turn away and find an alternative route, until eventually they made their way out of the zone that had been cordoned off. Amazingly, after all that had happened, Tom not only guided Mike to his meeting but got him there on time.

 *When the bomb went off, I thought about my wife and daughter. Tom just thought about getting me to safety. Without doubt a guide dog changes your life, but after our experience in London on 7 July, I feel I owe my life to Tom.*

Tom was named Heroic Guide Dog of the Year in 2006 for his bravery in the face of adversity. He beat competition from other nominated guide dogs from all around the UK in an event organised by The Guide Dogs for the Blind Association.

🐾 ROZ 🐾

Guide dog Roz was determined to carry out her duties to her owner, Gary Wickett, despite being badly injured in a brutal attack...

The inspirational and moving story behind guide dog Roz, a three-year-old Labrador-golden retriever cross, began when she was out guiding her owner Gary Wickett near his home in Great Barr, Birmingham. As the pair were making their way down a street in the area, Roz was suddenly savaged by a large dog, in a sustained and horrific attack. Gary was unable to prevent the attack or try to help Roz to defend herself from the much more aggressive dog:

> *Being totally blind, I felt completely powerless and could do nothing more than to hold tightly on to Roz's lead.*

The owner of the attacking dog did not try to help or stop it from happening, and when the dog eventually finished its attack and was brought under control, the owner fled the scene without offering any assistance to Gary or Roz.

Despite suffering from horrendous injuries and bleeding heavily, Roz still managed to safely guide her owner Gary the half mile home so that he was able to call for help for her. She was lucky to be alive, and it was thought that she would have to retire due to physical injuries which included four severe bite wounds, 13 smaller wounds and a badly damaged tail, as well as the mental trauma she would have suffered in the incident.

However, after hours in surgery having her injuries tended to and many weeks rest and recuperation, she was back guiding Gary to his workplace in the busy centre of Birmingham. She was able to walk with confidence down the same road where the attack took place, loyally providing Gary with life-transforming independence and freedom.

Although a police investigation followed, the owner and dog involved in Roz's attack were not found. Roz was crowned Overall Champion Guide Dog of the Year 2007 by The Guide Dogs for the Blind Association.

A history of leading the blind

Dogs are thought to have been used to guide the blind since at least as far back as the mid-eighteenth century. During World War One, the first guide dog training schools were set up in Germany with the aim of helping returning soldiers who were blinded in combat to regain mobility. Britain's first guide dogs were German shepherds, and the first three trained were given to veterans blinded in World War One. In 1929 the first US guide dog school, The Seeing Eye, was founded in Morristown, New Jersey, and in 1934, The Guide Dogs for the Blind Association was set up in the UK, with the objective of providing 'guide dogs and other mobility services that increase the independence and dignity of blind and partially-sighted people.'

 DORADO

To have been inside the World Trade Center on 11 September 2001 when the towers were hit by hijacked planes must have been a terrifying ordeal. For a blind man it must have been even more distressing. Luckily for Omar Eduardo Rivera, his faithful friend and guide dog Dorado was there to guide him out of danger…

Computer technician Omar was sitting at his desk with his guide dog, four-year-old Labrador Dorado, at his feet on the 71st floor of the north tower when the plane crashed into the building 25 floors above. As chaos ensued in the office, Omar could hear the sound of glass shattering around him and people screaming and fleeing. Smoke began to fill his lungs and the heat was quickly becoming unbearable.

Being unable to see, he knew that his chances of getting down the stairs past all the fallen obstacles and panicked, running people were pretty slim, and so he resigned himself to his fate. He let Dorado off his leash and ordered him to go, in the hope that at least the dog would make it out alive. At that moment Dorado was swept away by the crowds of pushing people, and Omar found himself alone.

But then, only a few minutes later, Omar felt a familiar nudging against his knee. His faithful guide had returned.

Dorado guided his master to the stairwell, where a co-worker recognised Omar. With his co-worker on his right and Dorado on his left, Omar was safely guided down 70 flights of stairs and out into the street. Because of the sheer volume of people on the stairs, it took them nearly an hour to get out, with Dorado nudging Omar reassuringly every step of the way.

It was only moments after they made it out onto the street that the tower collapsed. 'I owe my life to Dorado,' Omar later said, 'my companion and best friend.'

🐾 ROSELLE 🐾

Michael Hingson was another blind person who was in the World Trade Center when the terrorist attacks happened…

Yellow Labrador and guide dog, Roselle, led Michael Hingson down 78 floors and out of the World Trade Center after the planes hit. But her work didn't end there – she still had to get Michael safely home. When they were about two blocks away from the building, the first tower began to collapse. Amongst all the chaos Roselle remained calm as they ran for the shelter of the subway. When they re-emerged, the second tower collapsed, covering them with ash. But Roselle still remained calm, and guided Michael to the home of one of his friends, where he was able to wait in safety until the trains were back in action, then travel home to his worried wife. Since then Michael has become a motivational speaker, drawing on his experience with Roselle that day when he speaks to audiences about trust and teamwork.

SAVING OTHER ANIMALS

When a dog acts to save a member of its owner's family, or another family pet, it can be explained in part by canines' natural instinct to protect members of their 'pack'. Female dogs are known to be very protective of their young and it makes sense that their defensive instinct would extend to their perceived wider family. But what makes a dog leave the boundary of its own home to answer the distress calls of drowning kittens, or to rescue a joey trapped inside its dead mother's pouch? It is stories like these that truly highlight dogs' potential capacity to be instinctively aware of another living creature's distress and to treat that creature with the gentle care and compassion they might show their own offspring.

🐾 REX 🐾

Leonie was surprised one afternoon when her dog
Rex brought home an unusual present for her…

Leonie Allan was out walking her ten-year-old pointer
cross Rex one morning when she saw a dead kangaroo
at the side of the road near her home. Roadkill was not
an uncommon sight where she lives in Torquay, Victoria,
Australia, so she thought nothing more of it until later
that day.

That afternoon Leonie was busy working in her front
garden when Rex took up the 'pointing' stance typical
of his breed, which indicates that the dog has found
something. At first when he ran off Leonie was worried
that he had found a snake, but he then returned to her
and dropped a live joey, or baby kangaroo, at her feet.

Incredibly, the joey had survived the road accident that
had killed its mother. Rex had somehow sensed that the
joey was still alive in the dead mother's pouch, and had
brought it back so gently that it was unharmed and calm.
In fact, Leonie noted that the pair already seemed to be
good friends as she watched the joey jump up at Rex and
the gentle dog lick the little creature in return. 'I was so
surprised and delighted. Rex saved the day,' she said.

The joey was named Rex Jr and was taken to Jirrahlinga
Wildlife Sanctuary where he would be cared for until

he was 18 months old, then released into the wild. The director of the sanctuary, Tehree Gordon, commented on the remarkable nature of the rescue; not only that Rex acted so calmly and gently, but also that the joey didn't see him as a predator and was completely relaxed. She had seen many humans bring joeys into the sanctuary who had accidentally injured the little animals when they struggled and tried to break free. She said: 'It's a lesson that dogs can be raised to be familiar and compatible with wildlife, you just have to teach them right from wrong.'

Pointing the way

Pointer dogs are used by hunters to help them find game, such as hares and pheasants, once it has been shot down. The first record of pointer dogs in England is dated around 1650, when they were used to find hares for greyhounds to hunt.

They are so named because of the stance they take up on locating game; alert and rigidly poised, with the nose and tail pointing in the direction of the prey. They have been trained in this behaviour by hunters for years, but untrained dogs of the breed have been noted to take up the stance 'instinctively'.

 NAPOLEON

Alexandra didn't know what had got into her dog Napoleon when he suddenly ran out of the garden, across the road and dived into a lake…

Alexandra Breuer from Michigan was out in her garden when Napoleon, her two-year-old white English bulldog, dashed off and leaped into the lake across the road. Bulldogs are not very strong swimmers, and Alexandra wondered what had given Napoleon the sudden notion to take a dip. Next she saw the dog dragging a bag, which she assumed to be full of rubbish, out of the water and towards the house. But then Alexandra heard muffled meowing, and opened the bag to reveal six kittens. It seemed that Napoleon had heard their little cries for help and run to their rescue.

Sadly, two of the kittens died, but Alexandra nursed the surviving four back to health and took care of them for two weeks before she could take them along to the local pet adoption centre, where new homes would be found for them. Napoleon was greeted with applause down at the adoption centre – word had got out about his rescue, and a crowd of fans had gathered to honour the courageous dog whose fast action had saved four little lives.

 LEO

Another plucky dog protected a litter of kittens while a fire raged around the house…

Leo, a terrier cross, stayed inside his home in Melbourne, Australia, standing guard over his family's pet kittens until firefighters found the poor animals, rescuing them in the nick of time.

The firefighters, who revived Leo with oxygen and heart massage after he was brought out of the house, were impressed by his tenacity and determination to keep the kittens safe. They nicknamed the brave dog 'Smoky'.

All four kittens survived the blaze, and the family, who were also evacuated safely, were glad to be reunited with all their pets.

 MILO

Milo didn't have the best start in life. His first owners had abused him, leaving him seriously disabled. But that didn't stop him jumping to the rescue when he spotted another dog in trouble…

When Lynda Pomfret adopted her six-year-old dog, Milo, he wasn't in great shape – he had been horribly mistreated by his previous owners and had brain damage and injured legs.

Lynda was out walking Milo along the beach near her home in Appledore, Devon, when he saw a spaniel struggling in the water and jumped in to save the animal from drowning. Lynda said of her brave little pooch, 'He's not the sharpest tool in the box but he'll always be a hero to me.'

Milo was later honoured by subscribers to Saga Zone, a social networking site for the over-50s, as winner of the 'PetZfactor 2008' competition. He was voted the most heroic dog out of more than 500 pets that were entered into the competition by their owners.

JASMINE

In 2008, Jasmine the wonder mum adopted a fawn called Bramble, the fiftieth animal she had become surrogate mother to at the age of just seven…

Police found Jasmine abandoned in a garden shed and brought her to the Nuneaton and Warwickshire Wildlife Sanctuary in 2003. The little greyhound was shivering and desperately undernourished, and needed a lot of love and care before she could begin to trust the staff at the sanctuary.

Once Jasmine had made a full recovery, she began to demonstrate a unique talent for caring for other injured animals brought to the sanctuary. Director of the sanctuary Geoff Grewcock explained that greyhounds are usually an aggressive breed – which is why they are used for racing – and so he was surprised at the amount of affection she displayed for other creatures, particularly as she had been so neglected herself.

Since arriving at the sanctuary, Jasmine had cared for five fox cubs, four badger cubs, 15 chicks, eight guinea pigs, two stray puppies and 15 rabbits. 'She simply dotes on the animals as if they were her own, it's incredible to see,' said Greg. 'She licks the rabbits and guinea pigs and even lets the birds perch on the bridge of her nose.'

Greg recalled one incident when two puppies, a Lakeland-terrier cross and a Jack Russell-Dobermann cross, found dumped by a nearby railway line were brought in to the sanctuary. 'They were tiny when they arrived at the centre and Jasmine approached them and grabbed one by the scruff of the neck in her mouth and put him on the settee. Then she fetched the other one and sat down with them, cuddling them.'

Jasmine's fiftieth protégé, Bramble, was an 11-week-old roe deer fawn found semi-conscious in a field by a man who was out walking his dog. Jasmine instantly took the little fawn under her care, cuddling up close to keep her warm, making sure nothing got matted in her fur and showing her lots of love. The fawn was to be cared for by Jasmine until she was old enough to be released back into the wild. 'They walk together round the sanctuary,' said Greg. 'It's a real treat to see them.

Surrogate mothers

Jasmine may well be the dog with the most surrogate offspring to her name, but she's not the only canine to have displayed such an overwhelming and non-discerning maternal instinct.

Vasile Borza, a farmer from Hodisel village in Bihor, Romania, was shocked to discover that his pet dog Lola had nursed two piglets that he had left for dead back to health.

And Lisha, a nine-year-old Labrador owned by the director of Cango Wildlife Reserve in the Oudtshoorn area of South Africa, was credited with playing surrogate mother to at least 30 baby animals, including a porcupine, a hippo, two cheetah cubs and three tiger cubs. The animals were either orphans or had been rejected by their natural mothers.

HELPING PEOPLE WHO ARE ILL

Is a pet dog just what the doctor ordered? The company of dogs has long been thought to contribute positively to the well-being of their owners, and the medical and scientific community have increasingly come to accept that owning a dog can have real benefits for a patient's health. Various studies have shown how having a dog can help reduce blood pressure, increase the chance of survival in stroke victims, improve the receptivity of disturbed children to psychological treatments and help people with depression by raising their serotonin levels and adding structure and meaning to their lives.

Dogs can also be trained to provide specialised help to people with a wide range of medical conditions, whether that be by assisting a wheelchair-bound owner in everyday tasks, or by indicating the presence of peanuts to an allergic child.

Another area in which some dogs have proved to be skilled is the early detection of diseases such as cancer, or the onset of diabetes attacks and epileptic seizures. Research into exactly how dogs are able to do this is as yet inconclusive, but stories such as those in this section are by no means isolated incidents – there are many other such awe-inspiring tales from around the world.

And then there are the loyal companions that, when they sense that their owner is ill or see that they are injured in an accident, know exactly what to do: raise the alarm and quickly get help.

🐾 BELLA AND FRODO 🐾

Thirty-year-old Lizzie Owen says her two assistance dogs have made her life worth living…

Lizzie has a condition called Osteogenesis Imperfecta, also known as Brittle Bone Disease – she has had about 200 fractures and over 20 operations to repair broken bones.

66 *Due to my condition, I am rather short of stature, measuring just 3'4", and I am a wheelchair user. My father died in 1994, aged just 46, and since then, I've had spells of quite severe depression. I also get frustrated with my own health; I have one fracture after another, and can't make plans for the future. At times, I've wanted to end my life. However, simply by being there, my dogs have stopped me from doing anything drastic – I couldn't leave them behind!* 99

Lizzie would often fracture her ribs when she bent down to pick things up and, after learning about the charity Dogs for the Disabled, it occurred to her that having an assistance dog to help out might save her from having so many painful rib fractures. In the summer of 2000, Lizzie was partnered with her first Dog for the Disabled. Bella was a lovely little golden retriever with a gentle nature, and she and Lizzie achieved some great things together. In 2004, she graduated from the University of Leicester with a BSc in Physiology and Pharmacology.

> *Without Bella, I don't think I would have been able to do it. When the coursework was piling up and I was ready to quit, Bella was there to give me a nudge in the right direction. Bella gave me confidence.*

Towards the end of her degree, Lizzie became quite depressed, concerned about what the future had in store for her – she was just about to leave education for the first time in 25 years. She and Bella worked at Leicestershire Centre for Integrated Living, a local disability organisation for a time. However, due to an increased fracture rate, Lizzie had to resign from this job, and began to feel despondent again.

> *I felt really down, but Bella was always there with her smiling face and wagging tail to pick me up again.*

In December 2007, Lizzie had to have Bella put to sleep. The faithful dog was ten years old, and had been diagnosed with inoperable cancer. Lizzie hated having to make the decision to let her dog go, but poor Bella was in agony every minute of the day and, sadly, it was for the best.

> *She wasn't smiling, she wasn't wagging her tail, she was off her food – she was a very poorly little girl. I had Bella cremated, and her ashes are now buried in her favourite spot in Mum's garden. After Bella died, I wasn't sure if I could "love" another dog again. If I couldn't love it, how could I work effectively with another Dog for the Disabled? However, if I didn't have a dog, what did I have?*

In 2007, just before Christmas, Lizzie went to visit friends and family in Yorkshire, where she stayed with her stepfather's friend and his family. She spent most of her stay playing with their dog, Meg, and realised that she could love, live with and, most importantly, work with another dog. In March 2008, Lizzie was partnered with her second Dog for the Disabled – Frodo, a two year-old yellow Labrador retriever.

> *Frodo is a great young dog! His task work is superb! Not only does he pick things up for me and stop me from fracturing quite so many ribs, he also empties the washing machine, turns on lights, opens doors, picks up the post and helps me to undress. He's also a big comedian!*

Recently, Lizzie fractured her right femur. It wasn't healing, so she had to have surgery, but this was not straight forward due to her poor bone quality. Unfortunately, her mobility has been affected and Lizzie has been quite depressed since the surgery, but Frodo had a gift for making her laugh by clowning around. He prevented Lizzie's depression from deepening and, on the days where she felt down and didn't want to get out of bed, cheered her up with his antics. Frodo also carries out the crucial role of enabling Lizzie to live independently. They live by themselves in an adapted bungalow in Leicestershire. As well as his assistance dog duties, Frodo acts as a guard dog, and is always on hand in case Lizzie has a fall.

66 *Frodo is such a laid-back dog and nothing seems to faze him. I'm looking forward to what the future has in store for Frodo and me – maybe we'll do our Masters, hopefully we'll return to work. I may even get Frodo a passport so that we can go over to France! What I do know is that we'll have lots of fun together! Without my dogs, I would have had many more rib fractures, I believe that I wouldn't have got my degree, and I probably wouldn't be alive today.* 99

 ROCK'O

All parents worry about what their children eat, but especially Mrs Mers of Colorado, whose daughter Riley had a severe peanut allergy. Thankfully, Riley's dog Rock'O had a rare skill that helped to keep her away from danger…

If eight-year-old Riley Mers ate peanuts, or even touched something containing the tiniest amount of peanut residue, she would go into anaphylactic shock within six minutes and have to be rushed to hospital. Her doctor described her allergy as one of the worst cases he had ever seen.

Rock'O, a Portuguese water dog, had been specially trained to detect the presence of peanuts or peanut residue and warn Riley – and he was one of only six animals in the US able to do so. His job was similar to that of the sniffer dogs that track down drugs or bombs, but instead his target was peanuts. Whenever he detected a trace of them, he would sit in the 'alert' position, to warn Riley to keep a safe distance.

Rock'O's duties included checking out the school cafeteria in the first week of term to make sure that it was safe for Riley. Before she had Rock'O, Riley would have to wear gloves in the classroom, but with her faithful companion and peanut-alarm buddy at her side 24 hours a day she could relax a bit and feel more like a normal child.

Specially trained dogs like Rock'O are not easy to come by – Riley's family had to pay in the region of $10,000 to $15,000. Luckily, Riley's support network of family and friends managed to raise the necessary funds. The difference it made to Riley's life was definitely worth it.

CHUSLA

For years diabetic Elizabeth Wilkinson lived in fear of passing out and dying from a sudden hypoglycaemic attack. That was until she realised she had an unusual early warning alarm on hand...

Elizabeth Wilkinson, a mother of three from Southery, Downham Market, Norfolk, had been diagnosed with type 1 diabetes for over 40 years. Every couple of days her blood sugar levels would drop to dangerously low levels, causing a hypoglycaemic attack. Without instant access to carbohydrates she could become dizzy, collapse and even die. The attacks could happen as often as three times a week, and she relied on four daily insulin injections to control her blood sugar levels.

A few weeks after Elizabeth got Chusla, Bedlington-whippet cross, as a puppy, she was sitting on the sofa when the dog jumped on her and started nibbling the back of her neck. Shortly after she realised an attack was coming on – and that Chusla had somehow been aware of this. Since then, Chusla has detected several attacks in their early stages, and Elizabeth has come to rely on her as a warning system. Whenever Chusla did her warning 'nibbles', Elizabeth could quickly eat a few biscuits to ward off the attack – and Chusla would always gets a chocolate doggy treat as a reward.

Elizabeth's discovery changed her life – she could carry on as normal, knowing that if an attack was imminent, Chusla would be there to let her know, even if it happened when she was asleep in bed. Years before, Elizabeth had nearly died after she collapsed whilst out shopping and went into a coma. Chusla helped Elizabeth to conquer her fear of that happening again: 'I don't panic any more when I go out. It's really nice not to be constantly frightened.'

Elizabeth's 'little lifesaver' was registered as a 'hypo-alert dog' – one of just six in the whole of Britain with the ability to sniff out a hypoglycaemic attack.

🐾 PEGGY SUE 🐾

A couple who had planned a quiet afternoon in front of the television got more drama than they bargained for when their faithful dog spotted that her owner was in trouble…

Dorothy and Gary Geddings of Benton City, Washington, US, had settled in to their comfy recliners and were watching television when Dorothy felt drowsy and told Gary she thought she might drop off for a bit. Gary was soon dozing himself, with Peggy Sue, their Yorkshire terrier, nestled cosily on his knee, when he awoke suddenly to the sound of frenzied barking. Peggy Sue had leaped onto Dorothy's lap and was barking in her face. Gary was horrified to see that his wife had stopped breathing and was shaking uncontrollably in her chair, her lips turning purple.

He shouted to their downstairs neighbours, asking them to call for an ambulance, then tried to get Dorothy breathing again. Thinking ahead, he let their other dog, black Border collie Cassie, inside so she wouldn't get under the paramedics' feet when they arrived. But in an unexpected twist to this already distressing scenario, protective Cassie saw Peggy Sue on Dorothy's chest and lunged at the smaller dog, grabbing her head between her jaws. Gary managed to separate the two dogs and locked Peggy Sue in the bathroom for her safety, but she was already injured, with one eye dangling out of its socket against her cheek.

While Gary and Dorothy were at the hospital, their neighbour rushed Peggy Sue to the vet's, where she received an emergency operation to sew her eyes shut. The treatment cost $1,100 and the vet couldn't guarantee that she would retain her eyesight, even with further surgery, but the grateful couple didn't even consider having their little hero put down. She was soon back at home and adjusting to blindness – though she would occasionally bump into things, she seemed to manage pretty well, and her wagging tail showed that she recognised the voices around her.

Dorothy was prescribed anti-seizure medication to prevent her from going into a serious fit again – doctors at the hospital discovered that the attack was caused by scar tissue left behind in her brain after a benign tumour was removed two years previously. The Geddings didn't blame Cassie for attacking Peggy Sue: 'She was trying to protect her mama, too,' said Gary. 'She just didn't know how to go about it.'

Sensing danger

Alea, a cross-breed, was another dog who raised the alarm when her owner Maria Ardley collapsed in her bathroom from a brain aneurysm at her home in Lowestoft, Suffolk. Even though the bathroom door was locked, Alea was somehow able to sense from the other side that something was wrong, and rushed to get Maria's husband Steve to help. 'I knew Alea was special,' said Maria, aged 50, 'I didn't know how special. I am so proud of her.'

 ORCA

Cheryl suffers from a debilitating condition. Her Canine Partner, Orca, accompanies her everywhere, helping her with everyday activities. In 2003, though, one such activity quickly turned into a nightmare...

Cheryl Smith from York has lived with Reflex Sympathetic Dystrophy (RSD) for over ten years and uses a wheelchair to get around most of the time. She has been partnered with Orca, a highly trained assistance dog provided by the charity Canine Partners, since March 2003, and from the start he has been a tremendous help. One day, however, he proved himself to be more than a companion – he cemented his friendship with Cheryl, only a few months after they were first partnered together, by saving her life.

66 *We were out for the afternoon, when my wheelchair hit an uneven part of the path. I fell twenty feet down an embankment into a water-filled ditch which was at least a mile and a half from the nearest town. Unlike guide dogs, Canine Partners are all trained via voice commands so I gave Orca the 'Get Help' command and he immediately set off.* 99

Unfortunately, the first person Orca met thought the dog was a stray and tried to take him home, but luckily Orca slipped his lead. After rushing back to check that Cheryl was OK, Orca set off once more in search of help. This time he met a local jogger and, after barking and jumping around to get his attention, he led him to where Cheryl was lying in the ditch, the water level rising around her.

As soon as the jogger saw what had happened, he ran home to call the emergency services. A team of firemen arrived and managed to pull Cheryl to safety and, aside from mild hypothermia, she was unharmed. If Orca hadn't been there to seek emergency help, it could have been a fatal accident as Cheryl had already been there for well over two hours and was sinking in the mud.

66 *Since that day, my relationship with Orca has become even stronger and we seem to be able to read each other's minds. All I have to do is look or make a gesture and he knows exactly what I am thinking. I cannot remember what life was like without him and I actually feel quite naked if he is not by my side. The security he gives me is amazing and he has become quite a celebrity around the York area! Being in a wheelchair can make people quite shy around you, but having Orca changes all of that.* 99

As well as the practical side of things, Orca makes Cheryl laugh and cheers her up if she's feeling down. He throws his toys to Cheryl when he wants to play and even humours her by wearing the special rescue dog shoes she bought him to avoid his feet getting cut by glass when they go for a drink in their local pub.

He can even order my drinks. He takes a card up to the bar with my drink request and then the staff bring it over and I pay!

🐾 MADDIE 🐾

On a freezing cold night in 2007, Sam Good suffered a seizure from which she might never have recovered had it not been for her best friend Maddie...

Sam Good from Toledo in Utah, US, also suffered from Reflex Sympathetic Dystrophy, which causes major seizures and can render a person temporarily paralysed. One night she was almost ready for bed – the only thing she had left to do was to turn off the rear outside light, so she opened the door and walked across to the switch on the other side of the porch.

A recent cold snap, however, had lowered the temperatures to between −7°C and −10°C and the bitter cold of the night caused Sam to have a violent and sudden seizure. She collapsed onto the porch seat and just managed to curl herself into a ball to protect herself from the worst of the cold. She lay there for some time, in severe and unrelenting pain, and began to realise that, dressed in only her nightclothes, she was in danger of freezing to death.

She eventually mustered the strength to call almost inaudibly to her golden retriever. Maddie came running out of the house and repeatedly tried to rouse Sam from her seizure. When this didn't work, Maddie wriggled under Sam's body and lifted her onto her back and began to drag Sam back towards the house. For a dog that weighed just under 50 kilograms it was clearly extremely difficult, especially as Sam couldn't move to help her at all, even to hold on. But Maddie somehow managed to get Sam inside the house and pull her over to the bed. After a while, the warmth of the house meant that the seizure eased off, and finally subsided altogether.

When the nightmare was over Sam was grateful to Maddie for the great effort she had made in order to save her life.

MAX

Maureen was perturbed when her dog Max began acting abnormally. But it wasn't Max that she needed to worry about…

Ten-year-old red-collie cross Max had always been a playful and lively dog, so when he became withdrawn Maureen Burns knew something wasn't right. He began behaving strangely around her, sniffing her breath and then nudging her right breast and backing off.

Maureen, in her mid-sixties at the time, decided to check her breasts... and discovered a small lump in the right one. When a mammogram didn't show anything, Maureen convinced the surgeons to do a biopsy, which revealed that there was indeed a malignant lump. She later had two operations to have the growth removed.

Maureen firmly believes that Max saved her life. On the day of the biopsy she told the nurse that she already knew she had cancer, because her dear dog had told her. 'I thought she'd laugh,' said Maureen, 'but she said she'd heard it before.'

After the operations Maureen went back to her home in Rugby, UK, to be greeted by Max, who sniffed her wound and wagged his tail. He stopped sniffing her breath, and started acting normally around her again.

Maureen later became a supporter of Cancer and Bio-detection Dogs, a charity that aims to train specialist dogs to detect the odour of human diseases, including cancer and diabetes. A spokesperson for the charity said of Maureen's experience: 'This is not surprising to us. We have heard of dogs being able to detect melanoma or skin cancer on their owners.'

How can a dog detect cancer?

No one can say for sure, but one theory is that because dogs are descended from wolves they have the 'pack' instinct, meaning that the well-being of those they perceive as their pack members is tantamount to their own well-being and survival – so dogs are thought to have inherited the ability to sense when another pack member is sick, and this may include the detection of serious diseases such as cancer.

Medical studies have shown that patterns of biochemical markers have been found in the exhaled breath of patients; with their heightened olfactory sense, dogs may well be able to distinguish these markers and identify the presence of cancer. One study showed that dogs could detect the scent of bladder cancer in a patient's urine, while another suggested that dogs can identify the presence of and distinguish between breast and lung cancer just by smelling a patient's breath.

 CURLEY

Jean and her dog Curley had been best friends for two years when something happened that made Jean's parents realise just how invaluable a companion Curley was…

One night, ten-year-old Jean Stout from Long Island got out of bed feeling unwell and staggered out of her bedroom. She was having an acute asthma attack. Her parents were fast asleep in bed and would never have known anything was wrong if it wasn't for Irish terrier Curley, who barked loudly until Jim Stout got up and came to find his daughter unconscious on the bathroom floor.

Curley was later honoured with a medal from the Little Shelter Animal Adoption Center in Huntington for his loyalty. A plaque paying tribute to Curley's life-saving action was erected in the shelter's canine centre as a reminder of the heroism that animals can exhibit in times of need.

Sadly, little Jean died some time later from another attack – this time Curley wasn't able to save her. 'His eyes tell me how sad he is he couldn't help her this time,' said Ellen Stout, Jean's mother. 'He sleeps on Jeannie's bed every night.'

MEG

After one particularly violent fit which left epileptic Mark with severe facial injuries, his wife, Claire, decided to get him a dog in the hope that it would help to calm him. Meg soon proved to be worth far more than the £60 the Ryans paid for her...

Mark Ryan from Stafford, UK, was out walking Meg, a two-year-old Border-collie cross, just three weeks after bringing her home from the Roden Rehoming Centre in Shropshire when Meg started to behave oddly. She would weave between his legs and leap up at him, almost as if she wanted to stop him in his tracks. Mark, an epileptic, was trying to calm the agitated dog when he collapsed and had a seizure. Though he wasn't badly hurt, he was taken into hospital as a precaution.

Mark later realised that Meg had been trying to warn him, and began monitoring her signals. Whenever she became excited and started circling him he would find a safe place and brace himself to minimise the risk of injury during an oncoming seizure. Meg successfully predicted several serious fits in this manner since that first incident.

Mark said that Meg had given him his life back. 'Before I had her I was too scared to set foot outside for long periods in case I collapsed.' Having Meg by his side gave the former plumber the confidence to continue a normal life.

Dogs are able to detect changes in mood in other animals and humans, and can sense a rise in fear and adrenaline. Certain breeds, such as collies, form strong bonds with their owners, which allows them to tune in to their senses more easily. The majority of pet dogs would be able to predict that their owners were about to have an epileptic fit because of the change in body odour that would occur just before. However, Keith Dickinson, a dog behaviour specialist, has described Meg as a 'one-off', because 'most dogs would not react to it like this dog does: they would probably ignore it.'

Seizure warning system

Some scientists have suggested that the electrical activity that leads to a seizure begins in the brain up to an hour and a half before the patient demonstrates any outward signs. This activity is thought to take place in the part of the brain that regulates heartbeat and perspiration. With their acute sense of smell, dogs would be able to detect these changes.

🐾 FAITH 🐾

> Rottweiler Faith, who dialled 911 when her owner Leana Beasley fell from her wheelchair at her home, was a testament to the life-saving actions an intelligent dog can be trained to take...

Forty-five-year-old Leana Beasley, from Richland, Washington, suffered from grand mal seizures. At the Assistance Dog Club of Puget Sound (ADCPS), Beasley was helped by experts to train her four-year-old Rottweiler Faith to alert her to impending seizures by detecting changes in Beasley's body chemistry. Faith also learned how to call the emergency services by lifting the telephone receiver and pushing a speed dial button with her nose.

On the day of the accident, Faith's behaviour towards Leana changed: she became overly attentive, trying to stay in physical contact with her at all times. This wasn't the usual way that she communicated an impending seizure, so Leana wasn't sure what to make of it.

When Leana's wheelchair went over Faith knew exactly what to do, and she acted quickly. The 911 operator who took the call said that when she heard a dog barking persistently down the phone, she knew it was trying to tell her something. Faith kept on barking until help was sent, then unlocked the front door to let in the police officer who arrived.

Faith couldn't have predicted Leana's fall, but she certainly seemed to know something was wrong that day – when Leana was recovering in hospital, doctors discovered that her liver had not been processing her seizure medication properly.

🐾 BUNNY 🐾

Will and Cindy Sherman often took in stray dogs and cared for them in their own home; in fact, they had so many that looking after them was a full-time job for Cindy. Then one day they took in bulldog Bunny, who would repay their kindness by saving Will's life…

Bunny was in a bad way when she came to Will and Cindy Sherman from Tallahassee, Florida. A friend had found her abandoned at the side of a road. She was thin, weak and suffering from ear infections when she arrived at their house, and soon developed a nasty cough. Yet Will Sherman, 37, saw potential in her: 'I could see right away that she was the kindest, most crazily happy, appreciative animal I'd ever met.'

Will and Bunny soon developed a very strong bond – even the vet commented on it when Will took Bunny in for her vaccines and check-up. Will left the vet's and was just opening his car door to get in when he suddenly collapsed and passed out.

Bunny must have pawed at Will for a while, trying to rouse him – the doctors later found scratch marks around his neck. She then ran back to the vet's office, where she barked and scratched at the door to get the receptionist's attention. The receptionist looked out to see Will slumped over the wheel of his car. She called an ambulance and rushed over with her co-workers to help – by this stage Will was convulsing violently and foaming at the mouth. At the hospital Will was given a CT scan and the doctors told him he'd experienced a grand mal seizure.

It wasn't until a few weeks after the frightening episode that Will heard of how Bunny had gone to fetch help. Then it sank in – if she hadn't acted so quickly, the impact of the seizure could have been far worse: 'I'm used to rescuing animals,' he said, 'but to have an animal rescue me? Just the thought of it chokes me up.'

BULLET

Pam Sica was busy with chores downstairs when Bullet, the family dog, came to warn her that her baby was in trouble...

Pam Sica was making up her baby's bottle in the kitchen while her husband took a shower. The baby was in the bedroom upstairs, where pet dog Bullet was having a lie down. Suddenly, the dog ran into the kitchen, barking loudly. Pam couldn't make out what the dog wanted – he didn't seem hungry or want to go out, and kept running back into the hallway and waiting there.

When Pam finally went upstairs to the bedroom, she saw that the baby had turned an awful shade of purple and was gasping for air. Hearing her screams, her husband Troy came out of the shower and they tried together to get the baby breathing again. At first he thought the baby was choking, so he hit him on the back, then tried CPR. Luckily the paramedics came quickly after Pam had dialled 911, and were able to get the baby to Brookhaven Hospital and stabilise his condition. It turned out that the Sicas' son had double pneumonia and ASD, a hole in the heart.

Pam was convinced that if it hadn't been for Bullet, her baby wouldn't have lived. A few years before the incident, the vet had discovered a tumour on Bullet's liver. The Sicas couldn't afford the treatment and so had to borrow $5,000 to save their 13-year-old dog's life. But Pam Sica said that it was all worth it to save a friend who was such a big part of their lives, and who would one day save the life of their son.

🐾 TIA 🐾

Dogs are known for their loyalty, so perhaps it isn't so surprising to read stories of how they get help for their owners when they're in danger. But little Tia barely knew Sonia Rampley when she woke her in the night to warn her that her husband had fallen ill…

Sonia Rampley, 78, and Roy Rampley, 83, were dog-sitting five-year-old Patterdale terrier Tia and another dog called Fudge for two weeks as part of a local scheme where they lived in Norfolk, UK, called 'Barking Mad', which finds dogs temporary homes rather than putting them in kennels when their owners are away. Roy and Tia seemed to have grown quite fond of each other in the short time the dogs had been staying at the Rampleys' house.

The couple were asleep one night when Sonia was woken at about 2 a.m. by Tia, who was scratching frantically at her hand. She was so determined to wake Sonia that she had even drawn blood. Eventually Sonia got up, thinking the dog must want to go out. But when they got outside into the garden, Tia just turned and ran straight back in.

Confused, Sonia returned upstairs to the bedroom and turned on the light. It was then that she saw her husband lying on the floor. He must have been there for a couple of hours, and as there was no heating in the bedroom he would have been freezing cold. 'He was paralysed down one side,' said Sonia, 'he just couldn't speak or do anything.'

Sonia quickly called an ambulance and Roy was rushed to Norfolk and Norwich University Hospital, where Sonia was informed that he'd had a stroke. 'If it hadn't been for Tia I wouldn't have found him until the morning when it might have been too late.'

Worth their weight in gold

HJ, a three-year-old Weimaraner, raised the alarm when Loren Engelbrecht suffered a severe heart attack in the early hours of the morning at his home in Fredericksburg, Iowa. The plucky dog kept his owner company through his long recovery and was later given the accolade of a place in the Iowa Animal Hall of Fame this year.

Caleigh, a three-year-old Irish setter from Alliston, Ontario, went to fetch a neighbour when her owner, Max Lovett, collapsed in the snow after suffering a heart attack. Mr Lovett was barely conscious and hypothermia had already set in when the paramedics arrived: if Caleigh hadn't been there it would probably have been too late by the time he was found.

Lilly, a bull terrier from Orléans, Ontario, was just eight months old when she woke Jimmy Farrell from a deep sleep to alert him that his mother was having a heart attack in the laundry room downstairs. Ms Farrell put her recovery down to the actions of her clever pet.

ARCHIE

Archie, a bearded collie, was trained as a search dog, but one evening his handler Dave Patterson witnessed him helping someone in a way he could never have predicted…

Dave Patterson originally bought Archie as a family pet, but soon realised he was destined for greater things:

> *He was twelve weeks old and just a bundle of fluff with a small but very effective black nose. As he grew, his nose became one of his great assets and I came up with the idea that he could use it to help find people when they go missing. At fourteen months he passed his Lowland Search and Rescue Operational training and became the first search dog to be trained in Essex.*

Dave works for an organisation called Search Dogs Essex, which trains dogs to find missing people:

> *Part of our job is to raise money for the team by giving talks to different groups. I was asked to give a talk at a retirement home for disabled people and had taken Archie along as part of the talk.*

When they arrived, Archie immediately made his way across the room to a lady in a wheelchair and sat beside her. He nuzzled her gently and placed his nose underneath her hand, continuing to do so even though the lady didn't react to him.

> As I started my talk, I noticed the lady begin to stroke Archie, and quietly utter the words, "Good dog." When she spoke, her son, who was sat behind her, burst into uncontrollable tears.

Eventually, when the young man had regained some composure, Dave was able to ask him what the matter was. The man explained that his mother had suffered a major stroke nine years previously. The reason he was crying was not from sorrow but joy – his mother had been unable to speak since she had the stroke, and her words to Archie were the first she had spoken in those nine years. Dave was delighted that Archie had been able to gently encourage the lady's words just by showing his affection.

> The whole room cheered but Archie would not leave her side. Since then the lady has regained most of her speech and is now making up for lost time with her family. They say dogs help; well, Archie definitely helped this lady!

After six and a half years of service as a search dog Archie has now retired, though he still attends talks and gives demonstrations for schools and organisations around East Anglia.

66 *Now that he's retired he's got more time to spend doing what he enjoys – chasing pigeons off the vegetable plot!* 99

SAVING PEOPLE FROM FIRE

When a working dog is called to the scene of a fire in an official capacity, it is usually to help the search and rescue team locate people who were trapped when parts of a building have collapsed. In the UK, this work is done by the USAR: Urban Search and Rescue dogs. These dogs, usually collies or springer spaniels, receive specialist training for up to two years to develop their acute sniffing skills and wear a safety uniform, including protective boots and jackets. Speaking at a time when the dogs were first being introduced to the UK in 2008, Fire Minister Parmjit Dhanda said: 'These dogs are real lifesavers, as shown by their heroic efforts in all parts of the world. Their skills are crucial to giving the fire service the best possible chance of finding people alive in collapsed buildings.'

Canines are also increasingly used as accelerant detection dogs, professionally trained to detect flammable and combustible liquid odour residues in the aftermath of fire in order to help the fire investigator in identifying the cause.

Every so often, though, one hears heart-warming stories of dogs that have saved their owners or vulnerable children from a blaze. Without any formal training of dealing with fire, we can only assume that these dogs act out of some instinctive urge to protect others from harm.

🐾 ANNA 🐾

Early one Thanksgiving Day morning, Candace was woken by her dog, Anna, to find that her mobile home was on fire…

Candace Jennings was asleep on the couch of her mobile home in Idaho City. When she was woken by her dog Anna, a blond heeler, she had a terrible headache and realised that the place as full of smoke. Anna whined and howled at Candace until she got up and ran outside, but she decided to return inside; she worked as a janitor at different locations in town and wanted to retrieve her bunch of keys from her backpack.

Anna faithfully followed her owner back inside, where Candace quickly became disoriented and was soon in danger of passing out due to the smoke. She knew she had to get out, but in her confusion she crawled towards the pantry instead of the outside door.

That was when Anna began to push and nudge her towards the door, showing her the way out. Just as they made it out the roof collapsed and Candace ran over to some nearby trees for shelter. She had escaped with just some burns to her feet, but because she was outside in the nearly −10°C weather for sometime, wearing only her pyjamas she also developed frostbite. Little Anna and Candace's two other dogs were not injured.

Jennings had adopted Anna from an animal shelter, where she had been brought in as an abused and stray dog. Anna had now returned the favour by rescuing her owner.

In Port-of-Spain, Trinidad, the *Trinidad Express* ran a story about a dog named Rebel that had helped his owner safely escape a blaze in his home in time…

A blaze started just before 7 a.m. one Wednesday at the Marcano home in Warrenville, Cunupia. Lana Marcano, who owned the house, was out when the fire started, along with her other son, daughter-in-law and grandson.

Anderson Marcano was alone in bed and woke up on hearing his dog, Rebel, who was barking and tugging at his clothing. At once he smelled smoke, and realised his house was on fire.

After his own attempts to put out the fire failed he left the house, but the dog returned to the burning building.

There was no one else in the house except the family's pet parrot – perhaps Rebel went back in to try to rescue the bird. Sadly, the body of the heroic dog as well as the remains of the parrot were found after firefighters gained control of the blaze.

 UNNAMED DOG

One dog truly earned his place as part of the family when a fire engulfed the Breidings' home…

Jason Breiding was cooking in the kitchen at his home in Paducah, Kentucky, when a grease fire broke out. At first he attempted to contain the fire himself and told his family to get out of the house. His wife, Heather, grabbed their three-month-old son and quickly took him to safety outside.

The fire was soon out of control, however, and Jason knew he would have to leave it and get out. It was when he saw his wife Heather outside with their son that he realised their one-year-old daughter Samara was still in the house.

Luckily, Samara wasn't alone. The family dog was with her and gripped the baby girl's nappy in his teeth, dragging her to safety. He had been so gentle with Samara that she was completely unharmed. Though the Breiding family lost their home to the fire that day they were thankful that they all got out alive, and that their clever dog had been there to rescue their young daughter.

EVE

Eve was a loyal pet Rottweiler that pulled her grateful owner Katherine to safety after a terrible accident...

Katherine had just bought a used truck and was driving home that morning when it started to weave erratically across the road. So much for the great deal on the truck, she thought, as she managed to get the steering back on course, but then as she braked, there was a loud screech and the interior quickly began to fill with toxic fumes.

She would have been able to simply open the door and get away safely – if it wasn't for the fact that she was paralysed from the waist down. It was clear that the truck was at risk of blowing up, and she had to get out quickly. The smoke and fumes were getting thicker, and made it hard for her to find her wheelchair and then assemble it.

Eve, her Rottweiler, was still sitting in the passenger seat. She managed to reach over and open the door to let the dog out while she continued to fumble around in the heavy smoke. But Eve didn't go anywhere. Somehow, she knew what to do. The Rottweiler jumped back into the fume-filled truck, gripped Katherine's paralysed leg in its teeth, and dragged her out of the vehicle. The dog had pulled her ten feet away from the truck when it exploded into flames. The Rottweiler continued to drag Katherine to a ditch to protect her from the terrifying blaze.

A policeman arrived soon after and, seeing the vehicle on fire, yelled at the woman to get further away. Katherine knew she had to drag herself away from danger, but didn't have the strength. Eve seemed to have used all her strength also, and lay still. But the exhausted yet determined dog got up, and let her owner hold tight onto her collar while she dragged her another 40 feet away, where Katherine would be safe and could be rescued.

Canine fire safety watch

Three little dogs called Holly, Dudley and Little Ern were signed up by the fire service and specially trained to shut their owner in a designated safe room if they smelled smoke or heard alarms. When the fire crew arrived, they would then lead firefighters to the safe room.

This was as part of an initiative by Merseyside Fire and Rescue Service in the UK, who teamed up with Personal Assistance Dogs (PAD) to provide dogs that could help save vulnerable and disabled people from house fires. The dogs also learned how to press a panic button, put a towel by a door to help block smoke and use special alert signals to warn their owners of danger.

SERVING THEIR COUNTRY

Specially trained dogs have been used in military combat since Roman times. They would be kitted out with large protective spiked metal collars and coats of chain mail and sent into battle. In fact, the Romans are said to have had attack formations made up solely of dogs.

In World War One, European armies used ambulance dogs to help locate wounded soldiers on the battlefield. These dogs really captured the imagination of the public and they were fictionalised in many novels in the 1950s, such as Felix Salten's *Renni the Rescuer: A Dog of the Battlefield*. The British Army also trained up special messenger, sentry and guard dogs during the war.

The first ever 'disaster' rescue dogs were employed in London during the air raids of World War Two. The US also started up its official war dog program in 1944, when more than 10,000 dogs were enlisted for training (known as the K-9 Corps) over the course of the war.

Nowadays, dogs are used for a variety of purposes by military staff around the world, including sniffing out bombs and mines, and illegal weapons at border crossings; tracking suspected insurgents and subduing detainees.

 SGT. BODO

Joaquin Mello was on assignment in Iraq with K-9 Sgt. Bodo when an unsettling incident made the reality of war really hit home for Mello…

US K-9 handler Spc Joaquin Mello from Santa Cruz in California was in Iraq in 2009 with the 98th Military Police Company. He and an Air Force K-9 handler were completing a route-clearing mission near the town of Najaf for a convoy to proceed and were required to clear some suspicious rubble, which meant leaving the protection of the Mine Resistant Ambush Protected (MRAP) vehicle.

The pair divided up the task so that Mello would clear ahead of the convoy and the airman behind it. Mello and his dog, Sgt. Bodo, set to work together. Mello noticed that Bodo, a six-year-old German shepherd trained in explosives detection, was behaving oddly.

'I had Bodo on the retractable leash and while we were searching he started to get a little bit behind me so I tried to coach him ahead of me but he wouldn't go and I ended up getting in front of him,' said Mello, who knew by this unusual behaviour that something was bothering the dog. He leaned down to put his head close to ground level to listen, then gave the dog the order to seek. Strangely, Bodo didn't immediately comply.

'All of a sudden he jerked sharply behind me and him jerking the leash jerked my head up,' said Mello. 'I heard a whiz and a loud ping like metal hitting rock. Sand started kicking up in my face and I'm waving my hands because I can't see because I have dust in my eyes. Then it hit me like a ton of bricks – someone just shot at me.'

Mello had been completely unaware of the enemy close by and had no idea where the bullet had come from. The gunners realised what had happened and shouted to Mello to get back into the MRAP vehicle but he was momentarily blinded by the sand, so a soldier helped him to safety.

The bullet had landed only a foot in front of where his head had been on the ground. 'That was a scary day for me... If Bodo hadn't pulled me back it would have hit me right in the head.'

The likeliest explanation, according to Mello, for the dog's swift action was its powerful sense of hearing.

'He can hear things we can't. He will hear things before I hear them too, he lifts his head up, his ears perk up,' said Mello. 'It's possible he did hear the round and thought "dad's in trouble" and pulled me back... All I know is Bodo, without a doubt, saved my life that day.'

He was badly shaken by the experience, acknowledging that it was the first moment when the true reality of war actually hit him. Back in his unit, leadership asked Mello if he wanted to be put in for a Combat Action Badge after his close brush with fatal gunfire, but he declined.

'I just did my job. Bodo is the one who did something amazing.' Joaquin Mello will never forget the day his working dog Bodo saved his life.

All ears

Dogs have far better hearing than humans thanks to their immense auditory spectrum, which ranges from around 40 Hz to 60,000 Hz in frequency (humans can hear sounds of frequencies ranging from 12 Hz to 20,000 Hz). They are also equipped with mobile ears that can be tilted, rotated, raised or lowered to allow them to pinpoint the location of sounds rapidly, and can detect sound four times the distance away than humans can.

🐾 CHIPS 🐾

Probably the most famous and certainly the most decorated military dog was Chips, one of the first dogs in the K-9 Corps to be shipped overseas by the US Army during World War Two…

Dogs for Defense (DFD) was set up after the attack on Pearl Harbour during World War Two. The armed forces needed dogs, and thousands of patriotic pet owners across America responded by donating their dogs for enlistment into the K-9 Corps.

Chips was a German shepherd-collie-husky mix, and was donated by Edward J. Wren of Pleasantville, New York, to the K-9 Corps. Quick to learn, he was trained to be a sentry dog at the War Dog Training Center at Front Royal, Virginia, in 1942. Assigned to the 3rd Infantry Division, he would travel with that unit in North Africa, Italy, France and Germany with handler Private John P. Rowell.

One of Chips' first and most prestigious duties was to serve as a sentry dog for the Roosevelt-Churchill conference in January 1943. He was also credited as having been directly responsible for the capture of numerous enemy soldiers by alerting troops to their presence. On one occasion, Chips alerted his unit to an impending ambush then ran back to base with a phone cable attached to his collar, dodging enemy gunfire, so that the endangered platoon could set up a communications line to ask for the backup they so desperately needed.

During the 1943 invasion of Sicily, Chips and his handler were pinned down one morning on the beach by an enemy machine-gun team in a disguised pillbox. Chips broke free from his handler and lunged into the pillbox, attacking the gunners. He seized one man and all four Italian crewmen were forced to leave the pillbox and surrender to US troops. In the fight he sustained a scalp wound and powder burns, but later that night he returned to duty and helped take ten more Italians prisoner by alerting troops to their approach, giving enough advance warning for the squad to capture all of them.

For his actions during the war, he was awarded the Silver Star for Valor and a Purple Heart for his wounds, and was much lauded in the press; however, ironically it was the press attention that caused these awards to be revoked. The Commander of the Military Order of the Purple Heart complained to both President Roosevelt and the War Department that by so honouring Chips, they were demeaning all the men who had been awarded a Purple Heart. The dog lost his medals, but the unit unofficially awarded him a Theater Ribbon with an arrowhead for an assault landing, and battlestars for each of his eight campaigns. He was given an honourable discharge in December 1945 and returned to the Wren family in Pleasantville. In 1990, Disney made a TV movie based on his life entitled *Chips, the War Dog*.

Military heroes or 'equipment'?

The debate surrounding the awarding of medals to military dogs in the US not only led to denying dogs the proper recognition for their efforts, but also paved the way for the military to classify them as 'equipment'. Astonishingly, when the US pulled out of Vietnam, all 'equipment' was left behind, including the valiant military dogs, despite earnest efforts to bring them home. Stories vary as to what became of these trusting, loyal and devoted dogs which shared the danger with their human handlers.

 JUDY

British Navy dog Judy was credited with saving the lives of countless sailors during World War Two, and became the only animal ever to have been registered as a prisoner of war…

Judy the English pointer was a ship's dog on a Royal Navy vessel before and during World War Two, and gained a reputation for her skills in warning troops of the approach of hostile Japanese aircraft long before any of the human crew could hear them. Pointers were bred as gun dogs and are known for their alertness, and Judy saved the lives of sailors on many occasions in this way.

When the vessel to which Judy was assigned sank during a battle, its crew became prisoners of war. Judy somehow managed to get into the camp, where the conditions were terrible and the POWs had to work all day building a railway with very little to eat. The dog found scraps of food, which she would bring to the men, again aiding their survival. The Japanese prison guards tried to shoot her, but this time one of the men came to her rescue, a Royal Air Force serviceman named Frank Williams. Thanks to his efforts, she was registered as an official POW, becoming the only animal to do so.

Adopted by Frank after the war, she was smuggled back to the UK and awarded what was dubbed the Victoria

Cross for animals, the Dickin Medal, introduced to honour animals that made an outstanding contribution during the war. The following citation stands in tribute to her achievements:

> **"** *For magnificent courage and endurance in Japanese prison camps, which helped to maintain morale among her fellow prisoners and also for saving many lives through her intelligence and watchfulness.* **"**

She lived the rest of her life as a family pet. Her collar and medal were displayed in the Imperial War Museum, London, in 2006 as part of the 'Animals' War' exhibition, and in the seventies a book was published by Edwin Varley and Wendy James entitled *The Judy Story: The Dog with Six Lives*.

 **SAM**

Sam became the first army dog to win the Dickin Medal since 1944, for disarming a gunman while on duty in the Balkans…

When a gunman opened fire in the town of Drvar, which had been the scene of ethnic tensions in the Balkans in

1998, German shepherd Sam went in for the chase and brought down the suspect. Her handler, Sergeant Iain Carnegie with the Royal Army Veterinary Corps Dog Unit, from Melton Mowbray in Leicestershire, was on hand to disarm the man, retrieving a loaded pistol. 'Sam performed brilliantly – just like a training exercise,' said Sergeant Carnegie.

Sam also prevented a mob armed with crowbars, clubs and stones from attacking ethnic Serbs in Bosnia-Herzegovina six days later. The mob surrounded a group of around fifty Serbs, but the dog held them off until backup arrived.

'Sam displayed outstanding courage in the face of the rioters, never did he shy away. I could never have attempted to carry out my duties without Sam. His true valour undoubtedly saved the lives of many servicemen and civilians.'

Sam retired at the age of ten, and died from natural causes soon after. He was the 59th animal to be presented the PDSA's Dickin award since it was established by the animal charity in 1943.

SMOKY

Smoky first achieved renown for her actions as part of the US Air Force during World War Two. She went on to become a well-known entertainer back in the US when the war was over…

Smoky the four-pound Yorkshire terrier was found in the jungles of New Guinea in 1944, and sold to a dog-loving soldier named Bill Wynne. Bill went on to write a memoir, *Yorkie Doodle Dandy*, which tells how the dog became involved in the war effort.

Unusually for such a small dog, Smoky quickly became a member of the 5th Air Force, 26th Photo Recon Squadron, flew 12 combat air/sea rescue missions and survived numerous typhoons and kamikaze attacks.

Smoky truly became a war hero at Luzon airfield in the Philippines when she pulled vital phone wires through a pipe 70 feet long and only eight inches in diameter. 'Without Smoky, it would have taken the troops at least three days to dig up, lay wires and replace the strip, putting 40 US fighter and recon planes in peril of destruction by enemy bombings.'

Just as important, however, was the way she kept up morale among the troops, especially the boys recovering from wounds in hospital, by entertaining them with tricks to cheer them up. It was the start of a new career for Smoky, who returned to the US with Bill and performed live on stage and television for the next decade. This feisty entertainer lived to the age of 14, passing away in 1957, but she was truly a beloved dog hero and there are memorials around the country in recognition of her contribution to the war effort.

BAMSE

Bamse, a mascot for the Norwegian Navy, saved lives and carried out many heroic exploits during World War Two....

Bamse, a 14-stone St Bernard, was a mascot on the Norwegian Navy minesweeper the *Thorrod*, stationed in Montrose and Dundee at the time of World War Two. 'The average dog in my experience has a loyalty for his master and the family he lives with,' said Angus Whitson, co-author of a book about the dog. But, as Angus noted, Bamse appeared to have a loyalty for a wider family, and he looked after those he loved very well.

One of the many tales of this dog's heroic deeds describes how he once went into the water to rescue a sailor who had fallen overboard; another instance involved knocking over a man with a knife, who was trying to attack a young lieutenant. Bamse did not survive the war. The dog died in 1944 and is buried in Montrose with his head facing towards Norway. A statue in the town now pays tribute to the dog's heroism during the war; he was also awarded the gold medal for gallantry and devotion from the PDSA charity.

Angus Whitson and Andrew Orr pieced together Bamse's story and co-authored a book, *Sea Dog Bamse*, having gathered stories not only from the people of the town, but from Norway, Canada and South Africa. Whitson said that his favourite story is of Bamse taking the sailors out of the pub and making sure they got back to their ship on time. He said: 'From what I have read he physically pushed the sailors out of the pubs, there are stories of him nudging them along the road and anyone who tried to escape was herded into the crew again until they got back to the *Thorrod*.'

NEMO

Over 4,000 dogs served in Vietnam, saving thousands of American soldiers from death or injury, many of them sacrificing their lives in the process. And those which survived did not, like their handlers, have the freedom to come home afterwards. Nemo, however, was the first sentry dog to return to the US with honours after active service...

Nemo was a Security Police K-9 stationed at Tan Son Nhut Air Base in Vietnam in 1966. One day, Airman Bob Thorneburg and his K-9 Nemo had just gone out on patrol looking for enemy troops near an old Vietnamese graveyard, about a quarter of a mile away from the air base runways, when Nemo alerted him to something. Thorneburg immediately went to radio it in, but suddenly there was gunfire.

Thorneburg released Nemo and began firing as he charged towards the enemy, but the dog took a bullet, which entered under his right eye and exited through his mouth. After shooting and killing one of the Viet Cong, Thorneburg was knocked to the ground by a shot to the shoulder.

The determined K-9 did not give up the fight, however. In spite of the critical bullet wound through his head, Nemo launched himself at the Viet Cong and kept them at bay long enough that Thorneburg was able to call in backup.

Although the Quick Reaction Team's subsequent sweep of the area came up empty-handed, security forces used sentry dog teams to uncover two more groups of enemy soldiers.

Nemo, meanwhile, crawled to his handler to protect him further by covering him with his body, reluctant to let him go even when help arrived. Finally, both were taken back to base for medical attention.

Base veterinary surgeon Lt Raymond T. Hutson knew it would be a challenge to save the dog, and had to carry out many skin grafts to restore the animal's appearance. When Nemo had sufficiently recovered, he was put on guard duty again, although blinded in one eye.

It transpired that he would need further treatment for his injuries, and on June 23, 1967, Air Force Headquarters directed that Nemo be returned to the US with honours, as the first sentry dog to be officially retired from active service.

RAISING THE ALARM

Probably the most famous fictional dog hero character of all time was Lassie, originally created by the writer Eric Knight and then brought to life in numerous films and a long-running TV series. Lassie was always getting her owner out of scrapes, and if there was one thing the collie knew how to do it was somehow sensing danger and warning her human companions in time to save the day.

Perhaps the extent of Lassie's heroic acts painted a somewhat exaggerated picture, but there was something at the heart of it all that rang true, and won Lassie a legion of fans. This section gathers together a range of stories about the many real life dog heroes who have raised the alarm when their owners were in trouble, or led their owners to someone who was in danger and needed help.

BORIS

Many of the dogs in this book have received rewards for their acts of heroism, whether that be a pat on the head, a large bone, a lifetime of unconditional love or an official bravery award. But Boris, a dog from Devon, received something more unusual in recognition of his achievements – a rather special invitation…

John Richards was out walking his boxer dog, Boris, through the fields in November 2004 near their home in Ottery St Mary, Devon, when the dog suddenly ran off the path and stood by something he had discovered on the ground. John called him to heel but Boris refused. John continued to call him back, but Boris remained stubborn and it eventually began to dawn on John that the boxer was trying to convince him to look at what he had found, so he went back to where his dog was standing to investigate. What he saw filled him with horror.

A young woman, blue with cold, lay in the field; she was lifeless and still, and John thought she must have been dead. He called for an ambulance and a police officer arrived on the scene as well. Following procedure, the officer checked to see whether the girl had a pulse while John looked on and to their astonishment she did, although it was incredibly weak. An air ambulance arrived to take her to hospital; her heart stopped during the flight and she had to be resuscitated.

Eventually, after weeks in intensive care, 21-year-old Zoe Christie from Newton Poppleford made a full recovery from a severe case of hypothermia and was able to return to work as a care assistant. She was so grateful to Boris for saving her life that she invited him to her wedding as the guest of honour, where he received the applause and adulation of all the guests. Zoe's dad Trevor said, 'She owes her life to that dog and his persistence.'

SASSY

Teenager Andrea Vance was shocked by a discovery that her dog Sassy made in the pond outside her home...

Andrea Vance, a 14-year-old girl living in Dupont, Indiana, was at home with her mother and some friends. She decided to go outside and check what their dog, Sassy, was up to and found her crying and swimming in circles around something in the pond.

Initially, Andrea thought the small shape bobbing in the water was a doll, but when the tiny fingers clenched into a ball, she realised with horror that a baby had fallen into the pond.

She quickly fetched her mother, Cheri, and her neighbour, Terri Roark. While Andrea called the emergency services, the two women rushed over to the pond but at first they couldn't see anything. When Cheri spotted the doll-like form that Sassy had been barking at, she turned to the baby's mother, who was nearby, who looked over and then confirmed in terror that it was in fact her baby floating in the water.

Terri plunged into the water to rescue the tiny boy. The deep mud held her back but she eventually reached the infant, who had stopped breathing by that stage and turned blue, and was able to haul him from the water. Terri and Cheri performed resuscitation on him, and he eventually began to take gasping breaths again.

The baby survived his ordeal thanks to the efforts of Terri and Cheri, but they might not have found him until it was too late had it not been for Sassy raising the alarm.

🐾 DOR 🐾

Koichi Wada's dog Dor seemed to have an uncanny ability to sense when strangers were in danger…

Koichi Wada was out walking three-year-old black Labrador retriever Dor on a freezing winter night in

Iwade, Japan, when the dog suddenly began to bark loudly. She refused to continue on their walk, and instead went over to a metre-deep irrigation ditch. Her persistent barking led Koichi to the ditch, where he realised what Dor had found.

There lay an 86-year-old man, face up and submerged in water up to his ears. Since it was already dark and the temperature was so cold, it would have been very unlikely for the man to have been discovered before freezing to death if it wasn't for Dor passing by and pinpointing his location with her amazing skills of perception.

Koichi flagged down a passing car. As good fortune would have it, the driver was a doctor, who took the elderly man to his nearby practice and treated the injuries the man had sustained in the fall, which turned out to be only minor wounds on the hands and head.

The man made a full recovery, and Koichi was later awarded with a certificate of gratitude from the police for saving the man's life. A police officer commented that the certificate went to Wada because there was no precedent for awarding it to a dog. But clearly Dor was the hero of the day.

This was not the first time that Dor had been instrumental in saving a man's life. A year before the incident, Koichi and Dor were out for a walk when she started barking frantically at a parked car that was partly hidden under a bridge, prompting Wada to investigate and then call the police. Inside the car the police found a middle-aged man who was about to commit suicide and were able to prevent him from acting in time to bring him to safety.

CARMEN

Ivy Needham would have had no idea that her home was slowly filling with gas if it wasn't for her guide dog, Carmen…

Pensioner Ivy Needham was blind, deaf and had a serious lung condition. She had been making lunch in her kitchen at home in Belle Isle one afternoon when she unwittingly knocked the gas tap on her cooker. Gas began to seep out into the house and continued to do so for the next six hours.

The 83-year-old had collapsed in her armchair from the fumes when her guide dog, a black curly coated retriever called Carmen, began tugging at her sleeve to wake her up. As she has no sense of smell Ivy had no idea what was wrong; she just felt sleepy and groggy. She was relieved, though, that Carmen had woken her up, as it was time for her to have the regular dose of oxygen she has from tubes to help with her lung condition.

But Carmen, who had already been sick because of the fumes, was still intent on warning her owner of the danger. She kept trying to drag drowsy Ivy out of her chair and towards the door.

Luckily, at that moment Ivy's home helps arrived. As soon as they smelled the gas they got Ivy out of the house, switched the gas tap off and dialled 999. They then opened all the windows and doors in Ivy's house and managed to bring Ivy round before the emergency services arrived. Because Ivy had been taking in her oxygen supply at the time, she hadn't breathed in enough gas to make her seriously ill.

Ivy was grateful to all three of them for saving her life, but particularly Carmen. 'She definitely saved me,' said Ivy, 'She's my hero.'

Diva saves the day

In a more glamorous part of the world, an actress's pet dog alerted her owner to a gas leak. It was the day of the Golden Globe Awards and Salma Hayek had been suffering from a headache, so she went to take a nap before preparing herself to go out. However, she was soon woken by her dog, Diva, then realised that the gas was on in her house. The *Ugly Betty* actress later said that if it wasn't for Diva, she wouldn't have been around to celebrate with the rest of the cast when the popular TV series was awarded two Golden Globes that night.

ROLLA

Rolla was another faithful dog that was determined to warn her owner of impending danger…

It was 1820 and John Dodd, who ran a saddler's shop in Penrith, was driving his cart over the fells in Shap, Cumbria. Rolla, his faithful dog, was running alongside the cart. The weather took a sudden turn for the worse and a heavy mist began to descend. Suddenly, Rolla dashed out in front of the pony, forcing it to come to an abrupt stop. Dodd called to the dog to get out of the way, but Rolla studiously ignored him. Eventually he got down from his driving seat and went over to the dog. There, just behind Rolla, was the edge of a steep drop. If Rolla had acted a second later, John Dodd, pony and cart would have fallen over the edge and almost certainly to their destruction.

🐾 LANEY 🐾

A protective dog named Laney raised the alarm when a blaze started in the Peebles' family home one January…

Dave and Vicky Peebles had gone out to work, leaving their son Christopher and two friends, who were sleeping in the basement of their family home in Valparaiso, Indiana. Thirteen-year-old Christopher woke confused to find black Labrador Laney nipping his foot repeatedly. Laney would never usually bite, so Chris wondered what the matter was and got up to see if she wanted to go to the toilet. It was then he noticed that the house was filled with smoke. Thankfully, the children managed to run upstairs and get out of the house safely in time.

When firefighters arrived they found the home's garage and eaves on fire. The fire appeared to have started in an electrical heating unit in the garage. Though the fire caused $25,000 worth of damage to the house, Christopher's parents were just relieved that their son and his friends hadn't been harmed. 'She's always been very protective of him,' said Vicky Peebles of family hero and much-loved pet, Laney.

TYZA

A family from Kent had a lucky escape when their pet dog Tyza alerted them to a fire in their home...

A young couple were asleep in their home in Cliffe, Kent, UK, one Sunday when a fire broke out. Their pet dog Tyza woke them at 12.30 a.m. with her distressed barking.

When the couple woke they realised their bedroom was filling with smoke. They managed to get their baby and leave the house safely, though they later had to be taken to Medway Maritime Hospital to be treated for smoke inhalation.

A spokesperson at the local fire service warned that it was not advisable for people to rely on their dogs to wake them in the event of a fire in the home, and stressed the importance of having fire alarms fitted.

 FOXY

Many elderly people who live alone like to keep pets for company. One night in 2003, Joan Maguire discovered just how important a faithful companion can be…

Foxy, a seven-year-old pit bull cross, was run over by a car and suffered a broken leg as a result. She was operated on and recovered at the Little Shelter in Huntington, New York, but as an old dog who needed daily supplements for her leg injury and a part pit bull (a breed that has a bad reputation) it looked as though no one would ever adopt her. Eventually, however, 82-year-old Joan Maguire met her and it was love at first sight; Joan took Foxy home and they soon settled into life together. No one could have guessed how much of a blessing Foxy would prove to be.

Joan was leaving her house one freezing evening to take Foxy for a walk when she slipped on the icy steps outside her house and fell, landing awkwardly. She tried to get up, but her leg wouldn't move and she lay helpless on the frozen ground, becoming colder by the minute. She tried signalling to her neighbours with her torch but no one noticed it and she began to panic. Joan grew desperate as she realised that if she wasn't found before nightfall, she could die of exposure or hypothermia in the sub-zero temperatures.

Foxy realised that her owner was in pain and unable to move, so she spread herself across Joan's prostrate form in order to keep her warm. Then she began to bark to attract attention. But no help came for well over an hour. Undeterred, Foxy continued to bark, until a neighbour came outside to investigate the disturbance. They quickly called an ambulance and Joan was taken into hospital and treated for a broken hip.

The old saying goes that an animal once rescued never forgets the one who saves its life. Foxy had certainly repaid her owner's kindness and was honoured with the ProHeart® Hero Award from Fort Dodge Animal Health.

ProHeart® Hero Awards

The ProHeart® Hero Award programme was set up by Fort Dodge Animal Health, with the aim of honouring dogs that demonstrate heroism through acts of courage. Foxy was the fourth dog to receive the award. The first award was presented to the New York Police Department Canine Unit in January 2002 in recognition of their contribution at the World Trade Center disaster site. Other winners include Kaiser, a male German shepherd that had saved his family from a fire in their home; and Bullet, a male Golden retriever that alerted its owners when their baby stopped breathing.

GHILLIE

A morning stroll with her son's dog turned into a near-death experience for Mary Wilson…

The Wilsons lived in the Orkneys on the remote island of Fair Isle, off the north coast of Scotland. One morning 62-year-old Mary Wilson said goodbye to her husband and set off along the path away from the house with nine-month-old English springer spaniel Ghillie. She had reached a secluded part of the island when she suffered an epileptic fit and collapsed by the path, falling into the undergrowth.

Ghillie quickly set off to find help. After running for a few hundred yards, he came across a group of three engineers from Scottish and Southern Energy who were repairing a telegraph pole on a track, and he approached them and began to bark. At first, they thought he was behaving aggressively and began to back away, but after some time they realised he had no intention of attacking them and that he wanted them to follow him. They set off behind him and allowed him to lead them into the undergrowth. Ghillie took them straight to where Mary was lying unconscious but still breathing.

The workmen immediately phoned the emergency services, and Mary was taken to the road by tractor and from there to Balfour Hospital by ambulance, where she made a complete recovery.

Ghillie was later awarded the PDSA Gold Medal, the animal equivalent of the George Cross, in recognition of his determination to get help. Marilyn Rydström, director general of PDSA (the People's Dispensary for Sick Animals), said: 'His devotion and persistence that fateful December day undoubtedly saved Mary's life. This is an extraordinary story of that unique and inexplicable bond between people and pets.'

TAZ

Taz led rescuers five miles through the mountains to where his owner had fallen and lay badly injured…

The mountains of Moab, in Utah, US, are stunningly beautiful and also extremely rugged in places – the perfect place for an adventure athlete to train. Danelle Ballengee, a 35-year-old two-time world adventure racing champion and elite triathlete from Dillon, was doing just that with her dog Taz, a three-year-old German shepherd-golden retriever mix, in 2006.

They left their pickup at the bottom of their planned route and set off into the hills; Danelle was wearing a few lightweight layers, which she thought would be adequate clothing for the two-hour run she had planned in the

40°C weather. All was well until they reached Hurrah Pass, where Danelle's foot suddenly hit a patch of ice and she slipped, sending her tumbling over the side of the pass. She tumbled down three rock faces, each of 10 to 20 feet, before coming to a stop.

Danelle was unable to get up but managed to crawl for about a quarter of a mile in an attempt to find help before giving up due to the pain in her leg. Having resigned herself to spending the night outside, she began to do sit-ups to keep her body temperature up. Taz stayed with her the whole time and cuddled up, helping to keep her warm. But that first night wasn't the end of the pair's ordeal.

When morning arrived, there was no sign of rescue and she ate the energy gel she had brought with her on the run. During the day she sipped water from her bottle, and when it ran out she drank water from snow melt to stay hydrated. No one came to find her that day, and as evening set in she knew she would be in for another sub-zero night.

Meanwhile, a neighbour had phoned Danelle's parents to let them know that she hadn't seen Danelle for over a day. Though Danelle often went out kayaking or running without letting them know where she was going, her parents felt perturbed and decided to call emergency services. Search teams were sent out, but they had difficulty in knowing where to look, since Danelle hadn't left any indication of where she was going. After some time they found her pickup at the bottom of the trail, but there was still an enormous area to search and the search teams knew that she could be anywhere within that area. Then a remarkable thing happened.

Taz had run the five miles back to the pickup and, on seeing the search and rescue teams, began to bark loudly and persistently. The team tried to get close enough to identify him, but every time they did he moved away, barking again. They decided to follow him and he led them to where Danelle lay. They carried her down the trail and took her to hospital by helicopter, where she was diagnosed with a broken pelvis, frostbite in her feet, as well as internal bleeding and cuts and bruises.

Danelle's injuries required surgery, and it was predicted that she would not walk for several months, but if it hadn't been for Taz she may not have made it through either of the nights she spent out on the frozen pass, or ever have been found at all. As soon as she was able to, Danelle gave Taz the biggest hug of his life to say thank you for saving hers.

🐾 MAUI 🐾

Maui was a four-year-old bouvier des Flandres, a breed of Belgian retrievers renowned for their intelligence and protective nature. He displayed both of these qualities one Sunday when he played a vital role in saving his owner's life…

Leonard Fogg, from Edgartown on the island of Martha's Vineyard, off the East Coast of the US, decided to go for a walk down by the harbour in the late afternoon with his dog, Maui. As they strolled along, he spotted a boat for sale and stopped to look at it. Bending closer to see the details more clearly, he slipped on the dock and tumbled towards the boat, hitting his head and falling into the water.

He was briefly knocked unconscious, but he came round quickly as he was submerged in the icy cold water. Leonard had recently undergone a medical procedure which made it difficult for him to hold onto the boat for support, and he was unable to drag himself out of the water and back onto the dock. In his weak physical condition and with his clothes heavy with water, it was increasingly difficult for him to keep his head above the water. Realising that he would drown if he didn't do something quickly, he just managed to grab hold of a beam supporting the dock and hold himself partly out of the water. He was still in serious danger, though – he had no way of getting himself back onto the dock or onto dry land, and by now he had been in the cold water for about fifteen minutes.

Then he heard the faint sound of a dog barking, and what sounded like a man shouting 'Hold On! I'm coming!' When Leonard had tumbled into the water, Maui had continued to bark persistently and loudly until a patron of the nearby Wharf Pub came to investigate. Peter Robb, who had heard the dog's distressed barks while having a cigarette outside the bar, found Maui on the dock, pointing towards Leonard with his paws. Peter ran to the edge of the dock and saw Leonard still holding on to the support; he grabbed the freezing man's hand and pulled him along to shallower water, where he was able to hoist him out and onto the dock. Then, with the help of a couple of friends, he carried Leonard up to the pub and they stripped him of his wet clothes, piling assorted jumpers and coats on him to warm him up.

Leonard was taken to hospital and treated for potential hypothermia before being allowed home. Both Leonard and Peter agree that, if it had not been for Maui, no one would have known Leonard was in the water and he would have more than likely drowned or died from hypothermia. Leonard, who is diabetic, described how in the past Maui had alerted him to the fact that his blood sugar was getting low by barking. But his actions that Sunday had left an even greater impression on Leonard, and he planned to reward the dog with a tasty treat. 'When my wife was still alive we used to love to feed Maui prime rib. But it's been a while. So this weekend I think I'll go to the Square-Rigger Restaurant and get him a nice big cut. He's definitely earned it,' he said.

🐾 OSCAR 🐾

Jaime Garzon discovered that even small dogs can make a lot of noise when his little pug Oscar made sure he got the help he needed after he collapsed in the sun one day...

Seventy-four year-old Jaime Garzon's daughter Annie had taken in Oscar the two-year-old pug when he was a six-week-old puppy. Originally she had got the dog to keep her company as she stayed at home to care for her mother, but her father had quickly become attached to the little dog and they began to spend nearly all their time together. Jaime would carry Oscar in his hands when the puppy became tired of walking, and when Jaime drove, Oscar would sit on his lap with his little paws on the steering wheel. Jaime had recently retired and was having a hard time adjusting to life without work; Oscar seemed to motivate him and the pair often took walks together in the local park in Cypress, California.

During one of these strolls in Hettinga/Manzanita Park in 2006, Jaime collapsed from heat exposure. He lay face down on the ground, completely unconscious. Oscar climbed onto his owner's back and began to bark as loud as his little lungs allowed. After a while Beverly Martin, who lived in a house nearby, came outside to see what the noise was, and recognised Jaime. She quickly rang Jaime's daughter, Annie, who came immediately and took her father to hospital, where he was diagnosed with heatstroke.

The story might have been different if it had not been for Oscar; at Jamie's age, a prolonged spell unconscious in the sun could have made him very ill.

ACE

When Andrea Woodmansee became attached to an injured Border-collie cross that had been taken in by the animal clinic she worked at, she could have no idea just how much the dog would affect her life…

Richelle Gruber, a technical writer and veterinary technician, did volunteer work at the Salt Lake County animal shelter. One day a motorist called the shelter to report that a dog had been hit by a car. They took in the dog, a nine-month-old Border-collie cross, and tried to control its pain but couldn't do anything about his injuries until he had been claimed.

The days went by, and no one claimed him, so Richelle, who sometimes fostered dogs until they could find a home, took the dog to Wilson Animal Hospital, where she worked occasionally. The vets there found the injuries to be three fractures in his pelvis and four in his left hind leg. The ligaments of his right front leg were also torn. It could all be repaired.

High school student Andrea Woodmansee was then working at the animal clinic in her first job. She knew it was wrong to get too attached to the animals undergoing treatment, but it was hard for the teenager to resist falling in love with this poor injured and abandoned dog. She started calling him Ace.

Her parents were concerned, however, when she asked if she could bring the dog home at night while she tried to find someone to adopt him. Would their daughter be bringing home every stray she developed affection for? That wasn't what this job was supposed to be about. But Andrea had grown so attached to the dog, and as she reminded them, he'd be leaving for work with her every day. Poor Ace had been left homeless at only nine months old, had had a terrible accident and was such a loveable pup. They relented, but made sure she understood that it was only a temporary situation – she couldn't keep Ace at home forever.

So Andrea nervously asked at the clinic if it would be OK to help foster the dog. Richelle was pleased the teenager cared so much. She painted 'I love Andrea' on Ace's collar and gave him an ID tag with several phone numbers to call if he got lost.

Ace was responding well to treatment at the clinic but four days after surgery, a pin in his leg had to be moved. The vets wanted him to stay in overnight, but when

Andrea started to leave without him, he showed signs of extreme anxiety. She didn't want him to feel abandoned again, and it was a stormy night out there – perhaps that was affecting him too. Surely she could look after him better at home? The vets agreed. He could go home with her as usual but had to take it easy.

Unfortunately, it wouldn't turn out that way.

The rain was coming down hard that winter night. It's not known exactly how it happened, but her Mitsubishi Eclipse suddenly lost its grip on the road. It all happened so fast. The car sped off the edge and rolled down the steep embankment. Andrea was thrown from the car and landed at the bottom of the incline with a head injury, massive chest injuries and numerous broken bones.

A driver behind her had seen the car skid off the road, found a place to stop and called for help. The car and critically injured girl were so hidden down the embankment, however, that the emergency crew couldn't find anything. Was the driver sure there really had been an accident? They drove up and down and saw no signs.

Meanwhile, Ace somehow knew that instead of staying by his friend's side, he had to get help. In spite of his weak leg he made it up the hill and back onto the road, attracting the attention of drivers. He'd been hit by a car only a couple of weeks before, and should have been terrified of roads, but Ace showed amazing tenacity in venturing out into traffic. Two men stopped to get him out of trouble, and that's when he showed them to the car and the badly injured girl. Thanks to Ace, she was found and taken to hospital in time. And thanks to Richelle putting the identity tag on Ace's collar, emergency crews could inform all the right people.

As Andrea was being rescued, Ace collapsed on the road. It was only a short time after his last accident, and he was still healing from those injuries – now, in addition, it turned out he had a broken back, bruised lungs and internal bleeding. And yet with all that, he had still managed to go back out on the road to get help for Andrea. Thankfully, the break in his back was low down and it didn't go far out of alignment, and the vets said he wouldn't be paralysed – in fact, this strong young pup could be walking again within a week.

Andrea would be unconscious for some time, sedated during surgery, but she would pull through and learn what had happened.

As Andrea and Ace began the process of recovery and rehabilitation in their separate hospitals, and Andrea's parents Dave and Chris Woodmansee realised their daughter would be fine, they began to re-think the temporary nature of Ace's home. They told the vets to look after him well. It was clear that this extraordinary dog was about the best friend Andrea could have. Soon, it was settled: they'd all be going home together.

Mystery rescuer

In a similar story, when a woman's car sped down an embankment, a stray German shepherd dragged the injured woman up to the highway, and let her lean against him so she could summon the attention of passing motorists. Had the dog previously been trained in search and rescue work before? It's unlikely a trained dog would become a stray. But how does an untrained dog know how to rescue a human after an accident?

FIGHTING CRIME

Police dogs have come to play a hugely important part in fighting crime, and are involved in a wide range of roles: primarily their function is to protect their handler and enable them to carry out their job safely; they can also act as a deterrent; tracking dogs are used to locate a fleeing suspect; search dogs can help find a missing child; drug-detection dogs help sniff out narcotics; bomb dogs can detect explosives; and other dogs specialise in sniffing out hidden corpses or illegal weapons.

Any police dog handler knows that a working dog is much more than a 'tool' or even a trusted colleague: as many police dogs live at home with their handlers, they become a part of the family, and the bond between handler and animal can become very strong indeed. As some of these stories show, a police dog can be so dedicated to its role that it is willing to risk its own life in order to protect its handler's.

MAX

Once police dog Max had caught their scent, he was prepared to do whatever it took to track down two wanted criminals…

Dave Davies worked for 17 years as a police dog handler, based in County Durham. In the summer of 1995 he and his faithful colleague and companion, German shepherd Max, led a hunt for two wanted criminals who had abandoned a stolen car and fled. Dave takes up the story at the scene of the discarded vehicle:

> I went to the rear doors of the dog van and threw them open. Max jumped out and looked up at me with anticipation. He was the first police dog I had handled. He was a big, grey coloured dog with a long coat. He had a very laid back nature, almost to the point of laziness, until he was chasing some wrong-doer – then he came alive!
>
> "Head" I said to him, and he obliged, placing his great woolly head into the loop of the chain which I used to keep him in check by the roadside. The first thing I did was to cast Max around the stolen car to try to ascertain the direction these lads had taken. Casting a dog is

the term for asking it to search for scent of the suspects. Max circled the vehicle sniffing the ground enthusiastically.

When the dog has located a likely scent on the ground it sniffs around, and then suddenly flicks its head back to the area it thought was of interest, checks it again and, in Max's case, gives a big body shake. He always did this and it was a good clue to me that we were onto something. Max soon gave all these signs, and off we went. 99

Max and Dave followed the scent into a garden, whose owner came out to berate them for trespassing. When the man began to shout, Dave asked him to go back inside to avoid being attacked by Max, who became very defensive of Dave in tense situations. Once the man had gone, Dave instructed Max to continue his search.

66 *Suddenly, Max stood still, looking at me then at the ground and swishing his tail. A balaclava, still warm to touch, lay beneath a barbed wire fence leading from the garden to a steep river bank. Now I knew we were on the right track!*

We set off at speed down the bank. The river was very wide, rust coloured and extremely full; it had recently been in flood. I knew the river well and realised the current would be dangerous should these lads try to cross it. As we continued, Max would from time to time go to the water's edge. 99

About ten minutes later, Max started to pull very hard on his leash. When dogs do this, it usually means the scent has become fresher for some reason; perhaps the two lads had slowed down or taken a rest, then set off again. Max then switched from ground scent to air scent (the actual scent from the person being hunted; as the name suggests it is scent hanging in the air like smoke from a bonfire).

66 *We were getting close. Then a bark from Max – just one high pitched bark of excitement – and he dragged me towards a pile of tree trunks washed up by the river. Suddenly, I heard a crashing sound and a shout. Two young men broke from the cover of the tree stumps and ran for the river. Fully clothed, they jumped in. The current grabbed them and started to drag them quickly downstream. I recognised them both; they were prolific car thieves and small time drug dealers. To their credit, they were good swimmers; they didn't panic, just went with the current and swam across the river. I ran down the bank side requesting assistance over the radio, and asking for the neighbouring force to be alerted.* 99

The excitement was too much for Max. He could not understand why he and Dave weren't in hot pursuit of the thieves. In a flash, he plunged heroically into the swollen river and, with a 30-foot line still attached to his harness, he was swimming after them.

I tried to call him back; I didn't want to have to place myself at risk of drowning, I certainly didn't want to risk Max, and the line on his harness was highly likely to become snagged on the other bank. Max, however, was focused, and probably couldn't hear me due to the river. I stood up to my chest in water and watched in horror as brave Max crossed the river in pursuit of the two offenders.

The other side of the river at this point is a very steep bank, highly overgrown and heavily wooded. Max was still crossing the river when I saw the two lads crawl out onto the opposite bank. They ran at the steep wooded area, but they couldn't get through the thick undergrowth. One lad climbed a tree, the other scrambled at the bank trying to run alongside the river. I watched in dismay as Max pulled himself out of the river and went for the lad nearest to the water. I prayed the line attached to Max would not snag and that the lads would not hurt him. Max was very capable, but against two men with a plentiful supply of heavy branches he would be unlikely to be the victor.

The lad froze to the spot. Max barked at him. Then I noticed the other youth in the tree beginning to climb down. Max must have heard him, because he turned and ran at the tree making the most awful din I ever heard him make. Somehow the line did not catch on anything. Max continued bouncing between the two lads in this way for some time while I *tried to decide how to deal with the situation. We were in a very rural spot. I knew assistance was coming but it had to be by foot, and we must have been several miles from any road.* 🙶🙶

It was now that all the obedience training police handlers do with their dogs paid off. Dave called on Max to lie down and stay. He did so, even though he was about 150 yards across a river from Dave, with two criminals he was intent on detaining. Dave then instructed the two lads that if they felt able to safely swim back over to him, they should do so. Amazingly, they obliged. The two lads were so amazed at Max's skill all they did was sing his praises. He had been the hero of the hour.

Dave formally arrested and cautioned them both and escorted them to the waiting police car. They were charged with the offence of theft of the vehicle and several other offences they were wanted for.

Max's heroic efforts were later commended in court, and he went on to get an award for his exceptional abilities from the Chief Constable of his force.

🐾 LUCKY AND FLO 🐾

Lucky and Flo jointly sniffed out 1.6 million illegal DVDs in Malaysia as part of the biggest initiative against piracy the country has ever seen…

Lucky and Flo belonged to the US-based Motion Picture Association (MPA) and were loaned to the Malaysian government on a six-month anti-piracy assignment code-named 'Operation Double Trouble'. The black Labradors are the world's first dogs to be trained to identify DVD discs by the scent of the chemicals they contain.

The dogs are able to sniff out hidden DVDs that human search teams alone might not be able to locate – in one case they discovered a stash in a secret room behind a false wall. Once the discs are uncovered, the enforcement officers can establish whether they are legal copies or not. During the raids, Lucky and Flo helped to find 1.6 million DVDs and other optical discs, three DVD replicating machines and 97 compact disc burners, all worth $6 million, which led to 26 arrests.

'What they have helped us achieve in such a short time is remarkable,' said S. Veerasingham, Malaysia's deputy trade minister. Piracy is a serious crime which lost the DVD industry $6.1 billion worldwide in 2005, according to the MPA. 'Malaysia is committed to wiping out piracy and pirates,' said Veerasingham. 'We will go after them very fast.'

The plucky pair were honoured with a medal each and a hero's send-off before heading off back to New York to continue their work.

Sniffing around

A dog's sense of smell is estimated as being a hundred times more powerful than a human's. They have a far greater number of nerve cells in their nasal passages and a wider range of receptors; a dog is estimated to have more than 220 million olfactory receptors in its nose, while humans have only five million. The canine brain has a much larger area devoted to identifying smells than a human brain, and is dominated by the olfactory cortex, whereas the human brain is dominated by the visual cortex.

The mucus that keeps a dog's nose moist and shiny is vital to this process; it captures and dissolves molecules in the air, bringing them into contact with the olfactory epithelium inside the nose. Sniffing helps a dog to increase the detection of odours, by bringing more of the surrounding air into contact with the mucus on the end of its nose.

 **ANYA**

Neil Sampson and German shepherd Anya had only been working together for six months when the pair faced a violent and frightening situation together...

Police constable Neil Sampson is a police dog handler with the Wiltshire Police, stationed at the Force Dog Section in Devizes. In mid-2007, he was assigned a new dog to work with – Anya, a two-year-old German shepherd. She had only just finished her training as a police dog, and was very inexperienced, but she and Neil seemed to work well together and they had a good relationship. In early 2008, they were on their way to investigate a report of a confused elderly man in Swindon, when a call came over their radio to attend to an incident involving a man with a knife nearby.

They headed straight to the scene, where other officers were already in attendance and were talking to the person who had called the police. Neil decided to keep watch on the entrance to the flats where the incident had taken place, so that the man wouldn't be able to leave. The following is taken from Neil's report on the incident:

66 *I had been watching the entrance to the flats for a short while when I saw a man leaving the block and start walking away from them and me. The male was of such appearance that I called out to him, which resulted in him turning round and walking towards me. As the male was approaching I called out to him in an attempt to ascertain where he had been; he did not reply, but at this point I noticed what appeared to be blood on his trousers, which made me believe he was probably the male I was looking for.* 99

Neil called to the man, who turned around and began to walk towards him. As he didn't look aggressive, Neil didn't feel threatened, and he looked across to see where the other officers were; they were still talking to the first man, a short distance away. When Neil looked back towards the suspect, he suddenly realised that the man was carrying a knife. Neil asked him firmly to stop, but the man paid no attention and continued to walk towards him. Anya began, as she was trained to do, to bark loudly and strain on the lead that Neil was holding – usually this frightens a suspect enough to make them back off and cooperate. In this case, though, the man kept coming, slashing the knife in front of him as he did. Suddenly, the man began to attack Neil with both the knife and with his fist, punching and stabbing at him. Neil released Anya who jumped at the man and bit him repeatedly, barking and growling as she did so. The man slashed at Anya with his knife and she fell back, then picked herself up and carried on trying to defend Neil.

66 *I have only a slight memory of the incident after this point, I remember taser and parva [police methods of subduing violent people] being deployed and both failing to affect the male, then feeling a pounding on the back of my head and realising I was face down on the ground and hearing the sounds of a violent struggle taking place around me. I was not aware that I had been stabbed but soon became aware that I had been injured when, attempting to open*

my eyes, I found that one eye would not open and saw blood all around me; also, despite my best efforts to get up from the ground, I found that I was unable to. 🙶🙶

The man had violently attacked Neil and Anya, slashing and lunging at them in a frenzied assault, and Neil was stabbed seven times in the back of the head and the legs, causing severe injuries. Another officer was also stabbed in the face whilst trying to help him. Eventually other officers, from the armed response group, were able to restrain the attacker and arrest him with Anya's help. Anya had suffered a serious stab wound to her chest, which needed emergency surgery under general anaesthetic, but she made a full recovery from her injuries. Neil also recovered, but his injuries could have been far worse if it had not been for brave Anya's intervention. The following is an extract from the armed response officers' report:

🙶🙶 *It is the recollection of both officers that Anya remained focused on the offender, inflicting injuries that would subdue any normal person, however due to intoxicants and drugs taken by the offender, it is believed no pain inflicted could be felt and immense strength was gained.* 🙶🙶

Anya's bravery had not only been a major part of apprehending and subduing a dangerous and violent criminal – who was later convicted on several accounts of violence, including a charge of criminal damage against

Anya – but had also been instrumental in saving the life of her handler and in preventing any other officers from sustaining serious injury. Considering she had only been working as a police dog for six months and had never come across a violent situation like this before, her bravery and dedication to Neil were remarkable. The armed response officers' report contains a particularly poignant comment on Anya's courage, which demonstrates how grateful police officers are for the heroism of their dogs:

> *Her presence and assistance on this day and during the incident assisted greatly in ensuring injuries caused were minimised, and without her presence and determination 'to not let go and to protect' it is felt undoubtedly that the outcome could have been sadly very different.*

As a result of the incident, Anya was honoured with the ACPO Police Dog Team Operational or Humanitarian Action of the Year Award 2008 at the Crufts Friends for Life Competition, arranged by the Kennel Club. In 2009, she was shortlisted for the The Sun Hero Dog Award at the Dogs Trust Honours.

TRACER

Tracer, a German shepherd from the Police Dog Services Unit of the North Vancouver RCMP, Canada, proved to be an invaluable member of the team by assisting colleagues in dealing with a dangerous armed man...

On the night of 26 September 2000, Cpl Joe Arduini and two other officers from North Vancouver RCMP were called out to deal with reports of a man carrying a gun. When they arrived at the scene, the armed man was about two blocks away from Arduini and his colleagues and was walking towards them. Constable Christina Hughes and her dog Tracer were called in as backup and sent closer to the man's location to observe his behaviour. As Hughes was not in uniform at the time and the car she was driving was not marked as a police vehicle, she was able to do so without attracting the man's attention.

Hughes saw that the man was still advancing towards the three officers and was carrying a semi-automatic gun, so she radioed ahead to warn her colleagues. Arduini and his men acted fast, moving in to surround the suspect and instruct him at gunpoint to drop his weapon. When the suspect refused to comply, Hughes sent Tracer in to subdue him.

Tracer did as all police dogs are trained to do in such a situation, and bit the armed man on his left arm. Normally this would have been enough to discourage a suspect, but this man didn't seem to feel any pain from the bite. With Tracer's jaws firmly clamped around his arm, he lifted the dog up in the air and back down, and then pointed his gun at the dog's head. As the officers looked on in horror, he pulled the trigger.

However, luck was on Tracer's side – the gun misfired and the dog was called safely back to Hughes' side. The suspect then turned the gun on the officers, forcing them to open fire in self-defence. He was fatally shot.

Had Tracer not been there, it would have been much more difficult for the officers to evaluate the unpredictable suspect's state of mind and act accordingly. Tracer's presence that day meant that the officers could take action before the suspect hurt anyone.

 **BESS**

Ted Wright and his police dog, Bess, worked together as a team for many years. In that time, Bess was often called upon to help search for missing people…

Police officer Ted Wright and German shepherd Bess were called to Chatham, Kent, to help search for an 84-year-old lady named Elizabeth, who had been reported missing from a nursing home. Staff at the home were unable to find her when they tried to call her for lunch, so they notified the police. By evening, it was clear that the lady had indeed gone missing and the search team were alerted. The search was due to begin the next morning, so Ted and Bess set off very early to avoid the other search teams – it was easier and more effective for Bess to search unhindered by the presence of other officers.

They searched in gardens, alleys, rough ground, sheds and outhouses – anywhere in the immediate surroundings of the home to which the lady may have been able to gain access – but they had no success. Ted decided to do one last sweep of the area allocated for members of the public to search before nightfall.

> There was one alleyway that was completely separated from the nursing home by a very high wall. Access to it was from an adjoining street, although it was never used and was overgrown with thick brambles, nettles and rubbish that had been thrown over the wall.

Ted let Bess off her chain and asked her to search the alley, although he was not confident of any success in the dense undergrowth – he assumed the elderly lady would not have been able to make her way through the stubborn brambles. Soon Bess was working her way steadily through the alley, thorns tearing at her coat and skin. Ted followed, cursing and untangling himself every few steps. Suddenly, Bess gave signs that she could smell something. Ted told her to lead him to the source of the smell and they increased their pace through the brambles.

> **"** We had come to a sort of clearing that had a tree or two overhanging the path. There, where Bess was indicating, was the elderly lady, lying under a bush. She had obviously been there for some time. I crashed through the remaining brambles and told Bess to lie down while I checked her condition. I asked her some questions, but her replies came only as moans. I used the radio to direct the paramedics into the clearing, and the lady was taken away in an ambulance. **"**

Ted would not have seen the lady, hidden by the bush that had also sheltered her from the overnight dew, if Bess had not barked at her to let him know she was there. Her sharp sense of smell had located the lady's scent from some distance, and she had known where to look when she arrived at the clearing. The lady was entirely obscured from human view, and it is thanks to Bess that she survived to tell the tale of her ordeal.

The nursing staff had been informed of the successful outcome of the search and Ted and Bess were treated to tea and biscuits back at the home, which they drank as they pulled the thorns from their clothing and fur. Elizabeth had a check-up at the nearby Medway Hospital and was released soon afterwards to return to the nursing home. The staff reported that she looked tired but fit, and hadn't suffered any ill-effects. It was never discovered how she managed to get into the overgrown alley. By the time she was located by Bess she had been missing for around 27 hours – any longer and it could have been a very different end to the story.

JAKE

A dog that had an inauspicious start in life later went on to become a fully trained police dog and save a woman's life...

At seven weeks old, German shepherd Jake was left tied to a lamp post and was tormented by young children with fireworks. He was taken in by the Northumbria Police, and with lots of loving care and training he qualified as a police dog by his first birthday.

When he was three years old, he successfully located a 39-year-old missing woman who had collapsed deep inside some shrubbery near Harton Cemetery in South Shields, South Tyneside. She had only been missing from her home for an hour when the dog found her. The woman was taken immediately to hospital by emergency services.

'The fact the woman was found so quickly undoubtedly saved her life, as she was so deeply hidden you could barely tell she was there,' said PC Alistair Cairnie-Coates, Jake's handler. 'If she had been found much later, there could have been terrible consequences.'

Dog donates blood to save another's life

Did you know that all police dogs working for Central Scotland Police are registered blood donors? A cocker spaniel admitted to Broadleys Veterinary Hospital in Stirling was suffering from anaemia and had a very low red blood count. 'The dog was so ill that the only chance of survival was to carry out a blood transfusion,' said Sergeant Cameron Shanks of the police dog section. Luckily, the veterinary service was able to call upon Zak, a working police dog with the local force, for the blood donation necessary to carry out the transfusion. The cocker spaniel's life was saved and it was returned safely to its owners.

🐾 BANDIT 🐾

Police dog Bandit loyally defended his handler against a knife-wielding suspect in a dramatic confrontation...

Police were called to a home in Cape Breton, Nova Scotia, where a 22-year-old man had barricaded himself inside. The suspect was named as Ian MacDonald and was already known to police as being violent and aggressive. Corporal Rick Mosher and a four-year-old Belgian Malinois Bandit were amongst those called to the scene. As the officers waited outside for several hours for the emergency response team to arrive, MacDonald paced around in the garden, shouting and threatening the police. Suddenly, he left and walked off along the railway tracks towards the local store.

Mosher and Bandit quickly positioned themselves between MacDonald and the house as other officers moved in to intercept him, but he realised he was being cornered and made a run for the house. As he fled past, Bandit grabbed him firmly by the arm and refused to let go, dragging the struggling MacDonald around in circles.

It was when Mosher went to his dog's aid that MacDonald pulled out the knife he had concealed up his sleeve. As he swiped at Mosher's face with the knife, brave Bandit kept him far enough back to prevent him from harming his handler, but he bore the brunt of the attack in the process, and was seriously wounded. Seeing the danger Bandit was in, Mosher drew his gun and tried to call him off. MacDonald turned to attack the officers, causing Mosher to fire two warning shots. Bandit reacted to the gunshot by leaping at MacDonald again to protect his handler, and this time he was stabbed through the heart. Mosher fired at MacDonald, wounding him, but it was already too late. Sadly, Bandit died at the scene. A postmortem later revealed that during the attack Bandit's spinal cord had been partially severed – but even that hadn't stopped him fighting to defend his handler.

'I do not possess the words to describe how I felt watching my best friend knifed to death while he was valiantly trying to save me,' Mosher later said. 'Without hesitation, he leaped to protect me and received the deadly blow of a knife that was planned and meant for me… I truly believe Bandit's actions prevented innocent people from being killed or harmed. Bandit was a true hero.' A moving memorial service for Bandit was held and attended by many, including police service dogs and their handlers from across Atlantic Canada, and Bandit was later honoured with a place in the Purina Hall of Fame with the title Service Dog of the Year in 2001.

When MacDonald recovered from his wound he faced numerous charges – but because killing a police dog is not considered a criminal offence in Canada, he was never made to pay for taking Bandit's life.

FOLLOWING
THEIR INSTINCTS

There are some things in life that you just can't plan for. The lucky people in the stories in this final section were fortunate enough to have a dog on hand that reacted quickly when they found themselves in a dangerous predicament. These dogs seemed to know instinctively the right thing to do – whether that's because their reactions are quicker than ours, because of an innate ability to sense danger, a level of intelligence that we seldom credit them for or their instinct to protect, who can tell?

So far we can only guess at why dogs perform these heroic acts time and time again, but anyone who lives with a dog knows what exceptional creatures they are, and that each has its own unique talents and personality.

🐾 JILU 🐾

Mr Luo Ji-rong's dog Jilu acted quickly and selflessly one day when he saw a speeding car about to hit a little girl…

Akita Inu dog Jilu lived with Mr Luo Ji-rong and his family in Formosa, Taiwan. During the day he helped keep watch at a car pound on the east of Taiwan's main island where Ji-rong worked, guarding the property and looking out for any trouble in the area. On the day in question he was patrolling the pound as usual, when a car sped out of nowhere towards a six-year-old girl playing just outside the compound on the small road.

Realising that the girl was in imminent danger, Jilu ran as fast as he could across the road and leaped with all his might at the girl just as the car reached the place at which she had been playing. His paws made contact with her and pushed her sharply backwards and away from the road. Sadly, the car struck Jilu's back legs hard, leaving him unable to walk.

Mr Luo Ji-rong was incredibly proud of Jilu for the intense bravery he had displayed and wanted to help his beloved dog walk again. He said he refused to give up even if there was only a slim chance of helping Jilu walk, and that his family would love Jilu no less and continue taking care of him even if he were to remain paralysed.

An uncommon breed

The Japanese Akita Inu is a breed of large dog from Japan, thought to have originated in the Akita Prefecture. It is a separate breed from the American dog of the same name, and is rarely seen in other countries. They can grow up to 66 centimetres at the withers, and are red, fawn, sesame, brindle or pure white in colour. These striking dogs are renowned for their loyalty and intelligence. They love human companionship, but need plenty of exercise as they can become destructive when bored. They are good with children and quite playful, but have a reputation for being aggressive towards strangers.

DELTA

Dogs have been demonstrating their loyalty and protective nature towards humans since ancient times, as was revealed when archaeologists excavating Pompeii discovered the remains of Delta, a dog of unknown breed, next to those of his young master...

When Mount Vesuvius erupted in AD 79, lava covered the city of Pompeii, causing the death of most of its inhabitants. Delta, whose name was identified by markings on his collar, died alongside his owner, a boy called Severinus. From the position in which he was lying, archaeologists excavating the site were able to tell that he had been trying to protect the boy from harm when lava and volcanic ash descended upon the city.

A further examination of the collar showed that Delta had saved his owner on three previous occasions. The inscription described how the dog had rescued his owner from drowning by pulling him from the sea, defended him from four robbers who assaulted him and saved him from a wolf that had tried to attack him at the sacred grove of Diana. He faithfully stayed by his owner until the very end when the volcano erupted and smothered Pompeii, preserving the remains of the pair and leaving a lasting testament to their friendship. The remains of the heroic dog and the master he so faithfully protected are still on display today at the site of Pompeii.

RC

When two-year-old Vincent wandered out of his home in Canonsburg, US, wearing only a T-shirt in the early hours of the morning, he was lucky enough to find shelter from the freezing temperature with a neighbour's gentle dog...

Angela Harps was sleeping when her two-year-old son, Vincent Rhodey, got out of bed and went out of the house through a door that had been left unlocked, or possibly even open. Not only was the boy at risk of developing hypothermia due to the cold weather; his home was also situated near to an exposed drop onto a busy road.

The little boy was discovered by Terry Bard, who lived not far from the boy's home. Vincent was snuggled up and fast asleep with RC, Terry's German shepherd-husky mix, on the dog's bed of straw. It is unclear as to whether the boy had gone there of his own accord, or if the dog had found him and led him back, but one thing is certain: the boy was unlikely to have survived the freezing temperatures if it wasn't for the body warmth of the protective and gentle RC.

When police were called to the scene and found Ms Harp's door open, they took the situation very seriously and pressed child endangerment charges against her, though she did express deep regret at what she said was a mistake on her part. Terry Bard said that RC got quite agitated when Vincent was taken away to the safety of his grandparents' home – he seemed to have formed quite a friendship with the little boy.

UNNAMED
ŠARPLANINAC

On a bitterly cold night, soldier Frank Samardzija was on patrol when he became lost in the forest and made an unlikely acquaintance that saved his life...

It was 1988 and 18-year-old Frank Samardzija, serving in the Yugoslav Army as part of his compulsory National Service at the time, had been sent out on night patrol on the Macedonian/Albanian border. The temperature was –30°C and his uniform was woefully inadequate for protecting him against the freezing weather. He had no proper equipment – no torch or radio – and soon became disorientated in the forest.

It was then that he realised an animal of some kind was tracking him. Terrified, he pointed his rifle at where sounds were coming from and waited for the animal to move, assuming it was a wolf and readying himself to shoot it if it attacked. When it walked towards him into the moonlight he realised that it was a large dog with a long, thick coat – it was a Šarplaninac, also known as a Yugoslav shepherd dog. The dog wagged its tail and approached Frank, apparently delighted to meet someone in the wilderness of the forest.

He cuddled the dog for a while and noticed how warm it was with its winter coat. They walked together until they came across an abandoned house where they lay down, huddling together to keep warm. As they did so, Frank felt the dog's ribs poking through and realised it was extremely hungry. As he drifted into a fitful sleep, Frank felt the warmth of the dog penetrating through his cold skin and knew that he would die if the dog had not been there to keep him warm.

After some time, his patrol discovered him in the house and tried to lift him out – by now he was almost too weak to move. The dog, however, defended Frank from what it must have thought were attackers, and it was only after a while that the men were able to come and take Frank back to their camp. Sadly, he was not allowed to bring the dog with him or even to give it any food, and he never saw his lifesaver again.

The Yugoslav Shepherd Dog

The Šarplaninac (pronounced shar-pla-nee-natz), also known as the Yugoslav shepherd dog, is an ancient breed from the south-eastern mountain region of the former Yugoslavia, traditionally used for guarding livestock. They are large, heavily built dogs.

These highly intelligent and independent creatures can be trained to guard flocks without human supervision in high pastures, and they have a very protective nature; they have been reported to fight or chase off wolves, lynxes and even Balkan bears to protect their flock.

They are generally calm animals and are very gentle towards children and smaller dogs. When they are not guarding livestock they have been known to treat humans the same as they would their flock, herding them away from danger.

🐾 XIONGXIONG 🐾

Xiongxiong was only a small dog, but he used his brains and the full force of his little form to help his injured owner…

Mr Zhang, from Dalien, China, was at home by himself after his wife had left the house to run an errand. His refrigerator had been malfunctioning and he decided to get started on repairing it.

As he worked on the electrical components at the back, he accidentally brushed his fingers against the power outlet. They immediately cramped with the shock and a needle-like pain shot up his arm. His whole body began to tingle and he could not move to detach himself. The pain of being electrocuted was excruciating and the current passing through meant that he had lost control of the nerves in his hand. There was nothing he could do but scream and hope that someone heard him.

Alerted to his owner's distress by the screams, Mr Zhang's pet dog, Xiongxiong, ran into the room. He saw what was happening and quickly climbed onto a high surface and jumped onto Mr Zhang's arm. Although Xiongxiong was less than a foot tall and weighed just 10 kilograms, the force of his blow was enough to break Mr Zhang's grip on the live cable. Mr Zhang fell to the floor and waited for the pain and cramp to subside. After a few minutes he was able to move again and give Xiongxiong, who was waiting nervously to see whether Mr Zhang would be all right, a big cuddle to thank him for saving his life.

How the dog knew what he needed to do to save his owner remains a mystery, but his instinctive actions may well have meant the difference between life and death for Mr Zhang.

🐾 HERO 🐾

Hero, a four-year-old golden retriever, lived up to his name when his owner found himself in a dangerous predicament in 2002…

Gareth Jones, of Caldicot in Monmouthshire, Wales, was involved in a car accident in 1995 and had been paralysed ever since. He used a wheelchair to get out and about, and his assistance dog, Hero, was specially trained to help him in over 100 different tasks.

Gareth had taken Hero out for his daily exercise and some fresh air in the fields not far from their house one day when his wheelchair lost its grip in the muddy field and slipped, becoming stuck. No matter what Gareth did, he couldn't free the wheels and he began to wonder whether he would be able to get home – there was no one around to call for help and he felt very isolated and alone.

But luckily Hero was there and seemed to know exactly what to do. 'When I got stuck in the mud he realised I was in trouble, and started pulling on the rope I threw to him,' said Gareth. As Hero grasped the rope between his teeth and pulled with all his might, the wheels slowly began to grip again and the wheelchair started to move out of the mud. 'He didn't let go until I was clear – he knew exactly what he was doing.'

Hero was later presented with an outstanding achievement award for his actions at the All-Star Animal Awards in London by MP Ann Widdecombe. The plucky pooch is said to have solemnly offered the MP a paw to shake!

🐾 LA CHINA 🐾

A dog called La China captured the hearts of a nation when she saved an abandoned baby and cared for him as one of her own litter in Argentina…

When a 14-year-old girl from a shanty town near Buenos Aires gave birth prematurely to an infant she couldn't keep in 2008, she had no idea what to do. Panicking, she ran into a field strewn with litter and old boxes, laid the baby down and ran away.

Eight-year-old dog La China is reported to have heard the baby's cries in the field and gently carried the infant in her mouth 50 metres back to the den where her own puppies lay. Carefully, and without injuring the baby, she laid him down to sleep with her young litter, covering him with a cloth to ensure he stayed warm. When La China's owner heard the baby's cries, he rushed out to discover La China guarding the infant and making sure he was comfortable.

He reported his find to the police, and the baby was taken into care while they decided where he would live in the future. La China soon became famous for her rescue in Argentina, with the Argentine media comparing the story to that of Romulus and Remus, the legendary founders of Rome, who were said to have been abandoned as babies and rescued by a wolf nearly 3,000 years ago.

USEFUL RESOURCES AND INFORMATION

If you feel inspired by the stories in this book, you may be interested in finding out more about the charities and organisations mentioned.

Assistance Dog Club of Puget Sound (ADCPS)

The ADCPS is a non-profit organisation whose membership is comprised primarily of service dog teams and trainers living in the Puget Sound region of Washington State, US. The organisation acts as a resource for owners of service animals, providing mutual support for one another.
Website: www.dogsaver.org/adc

Barry Foundation

As owner of the breeding kennels of St Bernard dogs since 2005, the Barry Foundation's responsibility is the preservation and continued management of the three-century-old breed at its place of origin.
Telephone: +41 (0) 27 722 65 42
Website: www.fondation-barry.ch

British International Rescue and Search Dogs (BIRD)

BIRD is a highly trained team of volunteers, based in North Wales. Their aim is to alleviate the suffering of victims involved in disasters at home and abroad, providing a rapid response service involving the use of search and rescue dogs.
Website: www.birdcymru.org

Canadian Avalanche Rescue Dogs Association (CARDA)

This is a volunteer non-profit charitable organisation. Their aim is to train and maintain a network of highly efficient avalanche search and rescue teams across Canada.
Website: www.carda.bc.ca

Cancer and Bio-detection Dogs

This charity works in partnership with researchers from the Buckinghamshire Hospitals NHS Trust, who are supported by the charity Amerderm Research Trust. Their aim is to train specialist dogs to detect the odour of human diseases, including cancer and diabetes.
Telephone: 01296 655 888
Website: www.cancerdogs.co.uk

Canine Partners

Officially launched in 1990, Canine Partners enables people with disabilities to enjoy greater independence and a better quality of life through the help of specially trained dogs. Training assistance dogs to transform the lives of people with disabilities enriches human life in practical

ways such as dressing and undressing, supermarket shopping and vital emergency response procedures. In addition it provides physiological, psychological and social benefits that help keep people healthy and happy.
Telephone: 08456 580 480.
Website: www.caninepartners.co.uk.

Clay County Humane Society

The Clay County Humane Society is a private non-profit animal welfare organisation based in Florida, US, which was established in 1978 for the prevention of cruelty to animals, the relief of suffering among animals, and the extension of humane education.
Telephone: +1 (904) 276 7729
Website: www.clayhumane.org

Crufts

The world's largest international dog show held annually in London and organised by the Kennel Club.
Website: www.crufts.org.uk

Dogs for the Disabled

Dogs for the Disabled is a pioneering charity that trains dogs to carry out a range of practical tasks to assist disabled children and adults in order to achieve greater independence. The charity also provides a programme to support families with an autistic child. Since 1988 the charity has trained over 400 partnerships.
Telephone: 01295 252 600
Website: www.dogsforthedisabled.org

Dogs Trust (formerly known as the National Canine Defence League)

The Dogs Trust was founded in 1891 'to protect dogs from torture and ill-usage of every kind'. A 'small party of gentlemen', assembled by Lady Gertrude Stock during the first Crufts dog show, vowed to campaign for the protection of stray dogs and the provision of adequate veterinary care. They also vowed to campaign against muzzling, prolonged chaining and experimentation on dogs. The charity currently has 300,000 members and supporters.

Telephone: 020 7837 0006
Website: www.dogstrust.org.uk

Golden Retriever Rescue of North Texas

A charity rescue service based in Texas, US, that cares for neglected or unwanted golden retrievers and places them in permanent, loving homes. It also provides a facility for educating the general public about responsible pet ownership and the special qualities of the golden retriever breed.

Telephone: +1 (214) 750 4477
Website: www.goldenretrievers.org

Hearing Dogs for Deaf People

Hearing Dogs for Deaf People is a UK-based registered charity that selects and trains dogs to respond to specific sounds. Hearing dogs alert deaf people by touch, using a paw to gain attention and then lead them back to the sound source. For sounds such as the smoke alarm and fire alarm the dogs will lie down to indicate danger. Whenever possible, the dogs are selected from rescue centres, but they are also donated by breeders and members of the public, with the remainder coming from the charity's own breeding scheme. The charity provides a national service and no charge is made to recipients. Since its inception in 1982, Hearing Dogs for Deaf People has placed more than 1,500 hearing dogs.

Telephone: 01844 348 100
Website: www.hearingdogs.org.uk

International Hearing Dog, Inc. (IHDI)

IHDI has trained more than 950 hearing dogs since 1979 for persons who are deaf or hard of hearing. All of the dogs selected for this special training come from local animal shelters in the US.

Telephone: +1 (303) 287 3277
Website: www.ihdi.org

Lake District Mountain Rescue Search Dogs

A voluntary organisation dedicated to the training and use of mountain rescue search dogs to assist in the search for and rescue of missing persons, predominantly in a mountainous environment, but also in other areas where their skills may be of benefit. All Lake District mountain rescue search dog handlers are also members of a mountain rescue team affiliated to the Lake District Search and Mountain Rescue Association (LDSMRA) and therefore must already be competent in first aid and survival in a mountainous environment. The association

is a registered charity that can continue to exist only because of public donations.
Website: www.sardalakes.org.uk

Little Shelter Animal Adoption Center

This organisation is dedicated to saving all companion animals whose lives are in jeopardy. It is based in Long Island, New York.
Telephone: +1 (631) 368 8770
Website: www.littleshelter.com

Minnesota Society for the Prevention of Cruelty to Animals

Also known as The Minnesota Humane Society, this is a state-wide education, advocacy and rescue organisation dedicated to protecting the lives and interests of Minnesota's animals.
Telephone: +1 (651) 665 9311
Website: www.mnhumane.org

National Search and Rescue Dog Association (NSARDA)

The NSARDA is an umbrella organisation for Air Scenting Search Dogs in the UK. Its members are the Search and Rescue Dog Associations, which are located throughout the UK. Each of the individual Search and Rescue Dog Associations (SARDA) is a voluntary organisation responsible for the training and deployment of air-scenting search and rescue dogs to search for missing persons in

the mountains and high moorlands of Britain as well as the lowland, rural and urban areas.
Website: www.nsarda.org.uk

Nuneaton and Warwickshire Wildlife Sanctuary

The sanctuary is dedicated to caring for sick and injured wildlife. It takes in wild birds or animals with any injury and rehabilitates them, with the aim of releasing them back into the wild. The sanctuary also takes in small domestic animals that have been abandoned or mistreated, with the aim of rehoming them.
Telephone: 02476 345 243
Website: www.nuneatonwildlife.com

PDSA

PDSA is the UK's leading veterinary charity, caring for more than 350,000 pet patients belonging to people in need. They provide free veterinary treatment to sick and injured animals and promote responsible pet ownership.
Telephone: 0800 854 194
Website: www.pdsa.org.uk

Penrith Mountain Rescue Team

PMRT was founded in 1959 and is affiliated to the Lake District Search and Mountain Rescue Association (LDSAMRA) and to the national governing body – Mountain Rescue (MR). The team is manned entirely by volunteers who give freely of their time and skills to provide a search and rescue resource to Cumbria Constabulary. Their area of operation covers some 2,500 sq. km across

the Lake District National Park (north-eastern Fells), the northern Pennines and the Eden Valley.
Website: www.penrithmrt.org.uk

Search Dogs Essex

This is a non-profit voluntary organisation whose primary role is to assist the police and local search and rescue teams. They are available 24 hours a day and seven days a week for call-out to search for missing persons across Essex and surrounding areas. Their members are all 'Search Trained' to levels specified by the Association of Lowlands Search and Rescue (ALSAR) and the dogs are individually assessed to standards agreed by the Lowland Search Dogs Committee.
Telephone: 01245 381 988
Website: www.searchdogsessex.org.uk

The Animal Miracle Network

The Animal Miracle Network is a US-based virtual 'web of love', connecting with animal lovers, shelters, rescues and businesses that help orphaned animals find new homes through their participation in educational and family events.
Telephone: +1 (877) 205 0871
Website: www.animalmiraclefoundation.org

The Guide Dogs for the Blind Association (UK)

This organisation exists to provide guide dogs and other mobility services that increase the independence and dignity of blind and partially sighted people. They campaign for

improved rehabilitation services and unhindered access for those who are blind or partially sighted.
Telephone: 0118 983 5555
Website: www.guidedogs.org.uk

The Humane Society of the United States

This is the US nation's largest animal protection organisation. Established in 1954, the HSUS seeks a humane and sustainable world for all animals.
Telephone: +1 (202) 452 1100
Website: www.hsus.org

The Kennel Club

The primary objective of the Kennel Club is to promote, in every way, the general improvement of dogs.
Telephone: 0870 606 6750
Website: www.thekennelclub.org.uk

The Seeing Eye

The Seeing Eye Inc., is the oldest existing dog guide school in the world. Twelve times a year, as many as 24 students at a time visit the Morristown campus to discover the exhilarating experience of travelling with a Seeing Eye dog.
Telephone: +1 (973) 539 4425
Website: www.seeingeye.org

Urban Search and Rescue dogs (USAR)

The team was officially formed in July 2001 to give the UK Fire & Rescue Service a search and rescue dog team capability to respond to UK emergencies as well as overseas disasters. The teams are made up of firefighters from individual brigades throughout the UK, who are on 24-hour standby, 365 days a year.

Website: www.ukfssartdogteams.org.uk

Do you have your own dog hero story?

If you have your own stories of amazing canine bravery, we'd love to read them. Please send them to us at the address below and we'll include the best in any new edition of this book:

Ben Holt
c/o Summersdale Publishers Ltd
46 West Street
Chichester
West Sussex
PO19 1RP

Twenty
Wagging
Tales

Our Year of Rehoming Orphan Dogs

Barrie
Hawkins

TWENTY WAGGING TALES
Our Year of Rehoming Orphan Dogs

Barrie Hawkins

ISBN: 978 1 84024 755 8   Paperback   £7.99

'What a day! A dog from a car-breaker's yard on the loose with no lead and not even a collar, bathing a guard dog who had known me for an hour and trying to towel him in a room hardly any bigger than a cupboard, dirty water shaken all over me…'

This heart-warming and often hilarious tale follows a year in the life of Barrie and Dorothy Hawkins, who don't quite realise what they are letting themselves in for when they take on the challenge of rescuing and rehoming orphan dogs.

It seems every canine character has a surprise in store: Monty, the dog with a taste for cheese; Oscar, who has never been played with or walked but develops a new zest for life at the age of twelve; Digby, the enormous ex-guard dog who when he's not squashing the daisies is squashing Barrie's foot…

The husband and wife team welcome them all into their hearts and do everything it takes to change their lives for the better – and the lives of their new owners, too.

Have you enjoyed this book?
If so, why not write a review on
your favourite website?

Thanks very much for buying
this Summersdale book.

www.summersdale.com